# An Edition with Notes of Tennyson's "Maud"

# For OCR AS and A Level

CW00840118

# Josephine Pearce

## A Study Smart Guide
## © Purley Press 2017

I

1

I HATE the dreadful hollow behind the little wood,
Its lips in the field above are dabbled with blood-red heath,
The red-ribb'd ledges drip with a silent horror of blood,
And Echo there, whatever is ask'd her, answers "Death."

2                                                                              *5*

For there in the ghastly pit long since a body was found,
His who had given me life—O father! O God! was it well?—
Mangled, and flatten'd, and crush'd, and dinted into the ground:
There yet lies the rock that fell with him when he fell.

3

Did he fling himself down? who knows? for a vast speculation had fail'd,
And ever he mutter'd and madden'd, and ever wann'd with despair,                    *10*
And out he walk'd when the wind like a broken worldling wail'd,
And the flying gold of the ruin'd woodlands drove thro' the air.

4

I remember the time, for the roots of my hair were stirr'd
By a shuffled step, by a dead weight trail'd, by a whisper'd fright,
And my pulses closed their gates with a shock on my heart as I heard             *15*
The shrill-edged shriek of a mother divide the shuddering night.

5

Villainy somewhere! whose? One says, we are villains all.
Not he: his honest fame should at least by me be maintain'd:
But that old man, now lord of the broad estate and the Hall,
Dropt off gorged from a scheme that had left us flaccid and drain'd.              *20*

Synposis

The first five stanzas explain how the narrator's father was found dead in a hollow near his home, crushed under a rock. The death could have been suicide, as a business venture had failed and caused the father to lose his mind. The narrator blames this on the Lord of the Manor – Maud's father – who had exploited the narrator's father and ruined him, profiting financially in the process.

Verse form

The verses are quatrains, rhyming ABAB, but the number of syllables in each line is very irregular, between twelve and seventeen syllables. There are usually six stresses per line, which makes them known as "hexameters". Many of the lines use a central pause or caesura to create structure and rhythm, but when there are moments of high emotion, enjambment is used, or Tennyson breaks a line into three parts.

Stanzas 1-5

The opening "I hate" establishes the fact that the poem will be filled with powerful negative emotions, and this is picked up in "dreadful hollow". Tennyson establishes a key image of the whole poem – Blood – in a startling way by using personification. The landscape itself is like a monster with "lips" (line 2) which are "dabbled with blood-red heath". The repeated "d", "b" and "l" sounds, the key consonants of the word "blood", are repeated in phrases like "red-ribbed ledges". This is an example also of the pathetic fallacy, in which the landscape reflects the narrator's mood. Everything reflects therefore his morbid state of mind. The fourth line introduces an allusion to classical Greek mythology, with the nymph Echo being mentioned; we now use the word echo to mean a reflected sound. Here, though, Tennyson is using this classical allusion to make us feel the intensity of the narrator's horror when he remembers his father's fate. Whatever one says in this hollow is answered with the single word "Death" (line 4). This further establishes the mood of the poem as being obsessed with death. The fact that the word death is only an "eye-rhyme" or imperfect rhyme with "heath" further alerts us to the fact that things are not as they should be, and the natural world has become sinister and out of harmony.

The second stanza explains that the narrator's father was found in a pit on the heath. The pit is "ghastly" – like a ghost – an adjective which points to the fact that the father's memory haunts the narrator. The third line uses a series of past participles of increasing force; the father's body was "Mangled", an image taken from drying clothes, which means passed through a roller; this emphasizes how damaged the corpse was. The words "Flatten'd", "crush'd" and "dinted" are equally violent, and give a picture of the father's corpse pressed into the earth.

The third stanza introduces the notion of the "vast speculation" or business venture which had bankrupted his father. This drives his father mad. Lines 2-4 use alliteration in "mutter'd and madden'd" to describe how the father sounded in his despair, and the use of "w" sounds in line three, emphasizes another use of the pathetic fallacy to illustrate insanity, as the wind wails through the woods like a "broken worldling" or poor wretch, creating a very sinister sound. A beautiful metaphor of "flying gold of the ruin'd woodlands" means on the surface the golden leaves of Autumn, but here cleverly the word "gold" means also the money that the narrator's father has lost, ruining him and stripping him and his family of their future, as the woods are stripped of their leaves.

The fourth stanza uses enjambment between lines one and two to illustrate the "shuffled step" of people dragging his father's body into the house – the lack of smooth rhythm is emphasized in "dead weight" dragging behind them. This is also a pun, with the word "dead weight" used literally here. Line two also divides into three, to emphasize again the shuffling, haunted steps. The other images used in this stanza are those of ghost stories or gothic fiction; the narrator's hair stands on end, his heart almost stops as he hears his mother cry out. The alliteration of "sh" sounds in "shock", "shrill-edged shriek" and "shuddering night" focuses us on the piercing sounds of the mother's cry; shriek is also a powerful use of onomatopoeia here.

The fifth stanza opens with the narrator telling us that he is preserving his father's reputation. The main image in this stanza is horrifying, again taken from gothic fiction, and is that of a victim of a vampire. The old man – Lord of the Manor – has "dropt off gorged" from his financial scheme, leaving the narrator and family "flaccid and drain'd" – all blood drained away. This metaphor – of drained blood – here means they have been drained of all money and hope.

Why do they prate of the blessings of Peace? we have made them a curse,
Pickpockets, each hand lusting for all that is not its own;
And lust of gain, in the spirit of Cain, is it better or worse
Than the heart of the citizen hissing in war on his own hearthstone?

7                                                                               *25*

But these are the days of advance, the works of the men of mind,
When who but a fool would have faith in a tradesman's ware or his word?
Is it peace or war? Civil war, as I think, and that of a kind
The viler, as underhand, not openly bearing the sword.

8

Sooner or later I too may passively take the print
Of the golden age—why not? I have neither hope nor trust;                        *30*
May make my heart as a millstone, set my face as a flint,
Cheat and be cheated, and die: who knows? we are ashes and dust.

9

Peace sitting under her olive, and slurring the days gone by,
When the poor are hovell'd and hustled together, each sex, like swine,
When only the ledger lives, and when only not all men lie;                        *35*
Peace in her vineyard—yes!—but a company forges the wine.

10

And the vitriol madness flushes up in the ruffian's head,
Till the filthy by-lane rings to the yell of the trampled wife,
And chalk and alum and plaster are sold to the poor for bread,
And the spirit of murder works in the very means of life.                        *40*

Synopsis

Stanzas 6-10 show the narrator turning sharply from his own personal situation, instead raging against the age in which he lives. While England is at peace, with no foreign wars, Victorian society has become obsessed with gaining money. Family and normal life have broken down, and business has become corrupt. The narrator debates whether peace or war is healthier for society; this is a key theme of the rest of the poem.

Stanzas 6-10

Stanza 6 opens with a rhetorical question – the narrator does not expect an answer. He does not clarify who "they" are who talk of Peace, but he is very dismissive, using the word "prate", which means to talk idly and foolishly. Peace is personified as a female figure, but the "blessings" of Peace have been, paradoxically, transformed into a "curse". Line two picks up the "p" sound further in the word "Pickpockets", petty thieves who lust after the property of others. The harsh sounds let us know that the narrator is agitated.

The next line has another harsh sound, an internal rhyme with "lust of gain" rhyming clumsily with "spirit of Cain", again signifying agitation. Cain, son of Adam in the Bible (in the book of Genesis), killed his brother Abel as he was jealous that God loved Abel better. Cain was cursed by God to wander the earth. This reference prefigures the narrator's own fate in part two. The narrator then asks another rhetorical question: is "lust of gain" or the pursuit of money better or worse than indulging a people's desire for war? The strange metaphor of the "heart of the citizen hissing in war" (hissing usually means to sound like a snake, which in Genesis represented the devil) alerts us to the fact that the poem is more complicated than simply saying war is good, and peace is bad.

Stanza 7 criticizes the modern world as "days of advance", concerned with the "works of the men of mind". This means that technology and industry have advanced too far (see stanza 11 for an image of the Industrial Revolution), and clever but untrustworthy men have taken over society. No trust can be placed in a "tradesman's ware or his word" as old certainties have disappeared. Again, the narrator comes back to his obsession with peace and war, and he terms modern society itself to be a form of "Civil war", which means when a country is at war with itself. The shock of this thought is expressed in the very unmusical and severe enjambment between lines 3 and four: "that of a kind / The viler, as underhand, not openly bearing the sword". Modern society attacks the individual in a sly manner, not openly like a soldier.

Stanza 8 ironically uses the image of the "golden age", which is a mythical time of prosperity. Clearly the narrator thinks the modern world is far from a golden age. He fears that he too will "passively take the print" – a metaphor from printing, which means he will be marked indelibly – and be changed by the age in which he lives. He uses two strong metaphors – his heart will be hardened like a "millstone", and face turned to "flint" – to express how he risks becoming heartless like everyone else. Life is just "cheat and be cheated and die". He introduces again the main theme of death, in the words "ashes and dust." This echoes the lines from the Anglican Church's funeral service, "Ashes to ashes, dust to dust".

Again, stanza 9 introduces the figure of Peace, and describes her sitting under her traditional symbol of the olive branch. Here, though, she is drunk and maudlin. In modern life, and the modern city, the poor are "hovell'd and hustled together" in poor conditions, the alliteration stressing the squalor. They are "like swine", a simile that compares them to pigs in a farm. The line "only the ledger lives" is a metaphor from accountancy, where debts are written in a ledger book: this means that the only meaning in the world is making money. The final line is a very bitter one; Peace may be in a vineyard, usually an image of pastoral beauty, but "a company forges the wine". The word forges can mean manufacture in an industrial sense, but here it also means counterfeit or fake. There is no comfort or pleasure in this wine – it is not genuine, and has been corrupted by the desire to make money.

The tenth stanza uses a metaphor of "vitriol", which means sulphuric acid; here it signifies the madness which like a violent, corrosive chemical reaction, causes the "ruffian" or thug to beat his wife. It is sometimes used in modern English in the word "vitriolic", meaning violent or angry. The narrator then describes how basic food is corrupted, with chalk, plaster and alum – all white powders – added to the flour to make bread, in order to save money. This is the "spirit of murder" in the narrator's eyes; the closing phrase "the very means of life" refers to bread, which was often in the past known as "the staff of life", a staple food for the poor.

And Sleep must lie down arm'd, for the villainous center-bits
Grind on the wakeful ear in the hush of the moonless nights,
While another is cheating the sick of a few last gasps, as he sits
To pestle a poison'd poison behind his crimson lights.

*45*

When a Mammonite mother kills her babe for a burial fee,
And Timour-Mammon grins on a pile of children's bones,
Is it peace or war? better, war! loud war by land and by sea,
War with a thousand battles, and shaking a hundred thrones.

For I trust if an enemy's fleet came yonder round by the hill,
And the rushing battle-bolt sang from the three-decker out of the foam,
That the smoothfaced snubnosed rogue would leap from his counter and till,
And strike, if he could, were it but with his cheating yard-wand, home.—

*50*

What! am I raging alone as my father raged in his mood?
Must I too creep to the hollow and dash myself down and die
Rather than hold by the law that I made, nevermore to brood
On a horror of shatter'd limbs and a wretched swindler's lie?

*55*

Would there be sorrow for *me?* there was *love* in the passionate shriek,
Love for the silent thing that had made false haste to the grave—
Wrapt in a cloak, as I saw him, and thought he would rise and speak
And rave at the lie and the liar, ah God, as he used to rave.

*60*

Synopsis

Stanzas 11 to 13 continue the narrator's diatribe or criticism of the modern age, as he criticizes the newly industrialized world, and the way that people are cheated by the love of money. Again he notes that should war break out, the cowardly, cheating shopkeepers could not respond. In stanza 14 the narrator realizes that he is "raging" like his father. The narrator remembers his father's shocking death, and fears sharing his fate.

Stanzas 11-15

Stanza 11 uses personification again, much as the narrator had characterized Peace as a female figure. Here, the figure is Sleep. The narrator makes the image sinister as Sleep must "lie down arm'd", another image of war. Sleep is threatened by the "villainous center-bits", namely machinery for drilling. Tennyson uses enjambment here, so that the ugly verb "Grind" is placed at the very start of the second line with a strong stress, to emphasize how the awful noise disturbs people. The narrator is talking of modern industrial life, with machines running all night in the large towns of Manchester and Birmingham. In the middle of the 19th century other writers such as Friedrich Engels and Charles Dickens (in *The Condition of the Working Class in England* [1845] and *Hard Times* [1854]) had criticized the way that urban life in England had become harsh and unnatural. This is shown in the phrase "moonless nights", which are abnormal, the sky perhaps hidden by smog. The rest of stanza 11 is concerned again with the way ordinary people are cheated by shopkeepers, this time a pharmacist. The chemist "sits/To pestle a poison'd poison behind his crimson lights". The "p" sounds and the unnecessary repetition (or tautology) of the word "poison" make us imagine the awful grinding sound of the pestle in the mortar as he makes his bogus drugs.

Stanza 12 continues with social criticism, of mothers who kill their children for handouts – the "burial fee". Tennyson uses another biblical allusion. The narrator calls a mother a "Mammonite", which is a worshipper of money. It is also a grim pun on "mama" or mother. The narrator then uses hyperbole or overstatement, linking Mammon with another figure in "Timour-Mammon". This is an allusion to Timur or Tamburlaine, a 14th century Mongol warlord who conquered much of Asia and the Middle East. He became famous in the 16th century due to a play by Christopher Marlowe, and he was known for his cruelty. Here he sits on a "pile of children's bones", a powerful image, but one that is obviously symbolic or allegorical, not a real description. Infant mortality rates were very high in the mid-19th century, especially in the slums of industrial cities, and this is one source of this allusion.

The rest of stanzas 12 and 13 contrast this situation with war again, and are very explicit in telling us the narrator's preference (line 47): "Is it peace or war? Better, war!" Again the narrator uses hyperbole, talking of "a thousand battles" and "shaking a hundred thrones". In stanza 13 the narrator introduces the comic image of a "smoothfaced snubnosed rogue" who is so frightened by a "three decker" or warship from an "enemy's fleet" that he leaps from behind his "shop counter and till" and wishes to run home. The narrator cannot keep himself from dropping in another image of cheating businessmen, talking of the shopkeeper's "cheating yard-wand", or false measuring stick so he can trick his customers and give them too little. This stanza ends with a fifteen-syllable line broken into four very irregular parts – this clever technique expresses how agitated the narrator has become, as the line "And strike, if he could, were it but with his cheating yard-wand, home" is very ugly and difficult to say.

The narrator realizes this agitation in the start of stanza 14, where he seems to come to his senses: "What! am I raging alone as my father raged in his mood". The pause in the rhythm after "alone" – a caesura – and the balanced syntax show him regaining control, but only momentarily. Again, death enters the poem, as the narrator contemplates whether he should kill himself as his father did, rather than try to master his emotions; the repeated "d" sounds in line two of stanza 14 ("dash", "down" and "die") signal more anguish, and more violent emotion. The narrator introduces again Maud's father as the "wretched swindler" who has ruined the narrator's family.

The narrator feels increasingly sorry for himself in stanza 15, where he returns to the imagery of stanza 4. He asks "Would there be sorrow for *me*?" These thoughts foreshadow part two, where the narrator, in a mental hospital, imagines himself already dead. His mother's "passionate shriek" at seeing his father's body at least showed her love, and that someone cared for him. The narrator's father's body was a "silent thing", a very sad and poignant way to describe a dead body. The last two lines of stanza 15 again show Tennyson's use of the imagery of gothic horror, as the narrator imagines that the body "Wrapt in a cloak" would "rise and speak" and "rave" at Maud's father. The repetition of "rave" in line 60, at the very start and end of the line, show the obsession of the narrator – he, like his father, cannot escape from brooding on the past, even though it will inevitably lead to madness.

I am sick of the Hall and the hill, I am sick of the moor and the main.
Why should I stay? can a sweeter chance ever come to me here?
O, having the nerves of motion as well as the nerves of pain,
Were it not wise if I fled from the place and the pit and the fear?

*65*

Workmen up at the Hall!—they are coming back from abroad;
The dark old place will be gilt by the touch of a millionnaire:
I have heard, I know not whence, of the singular beauty of Maud;
I play'd with the girl when a child; she promised then to be fair.

Maud with her venturous climbings and tumbles and childish escapes,
Maud the delight of the village, the ringing joy of the Hall,                      *70*
Maud with her sweet purse-mouth when my father dangled the grapes,
Maud the beloved of my mother, the moon-faced darling of all,—

What is she now? My dreams are bad. She may bring me a curse.
No, there is fatter game on the moor; she will let me alone.
Thanks, for the fiend best knows whether woman or man be the worse.   *75*
I will bury myself in myself, and the Devil may pipe to his own.

Synopsis

Stanzas 16-19 complete the first part of the poem. The narrator thinks about leaving his home. He then notices that the Hall – where the Lord of the Manor lives – is being renovated for the family's return, and the return of Maud. The narrator remembers Maud as a child, and her beauty and popularity, but seems to reject all thoughts of her, and decides to continue in his solitude, turning inwards.

Stanzas 16-19

Stanza 16 opens with a very balanced line, after all of the intensely difficult verse of the previous stanzas, showing the narrator trying to re-establish his sanity in calm, measured statements. He is sick of "the Hall and the hill" – Maud's home contrasted with his own home – as well as "the moor and the main", namely the heath and the seaside. The repeated "h" sounds in the first half of the line (known as a "hemistich") are balanced by the "m" sounds in the second. This is very pleasing to the ear, and gives us hope that he can pull himself together, in spite of being sick of the place. The narrator asks himself a rhetorical question – "Why should I stay?" and in the following question, "can a sweeter chance ever come to me here?" is the first inkling that he might find a positive aim in life. But he still sees his home in terms of horror, and asks whether it is wise to stay with "the place and the pit and the fear", bringing us back to the site of his father's death. He acknowledges that he has "nerves of pain" – a possible mental frailty – so remaining there seems unhealthy and inexplicable, but thoughts of travel worry him too.

The next stanza brings, for the first time, the real reason why he cannot drag himself away; Maud, the Lord of the Manor's daughter. The narrator is fascinated by the Hall – and the exclamation mark after the opening "Workmen up at the Hall!" shows his interest. The inhabitants are coming back from abroad and the "dark old place" will be "gilt by the touch of a Millionaire". This metaphor means it will be gilded or made golden, or lit up, by the return of the rich owners, but the word "gilt" sounds like "guilt": Maud's father was guilty of the death of the narrator's father. This shows how death is never far from the narrator's mind. The narrator claims that he doesn't know where he has heard of the "singular beauty" of Maud, which is odd, and perhaps signals that he is hiding the extent of his interest in Maud, even from himself. We learn that he used to play with Maud as a child, and that she "promised then to be fair" – she had the potential to be very beautiful.

Stanza 18 suddenly shows the extent of the narrator's growing obsession with Maud. Every single line starts with her name, as he is overwhelmed by memories of her. She was a brave and lively child, and the imagery is equally lively and positive, with adjectives such as "venturous", "sweet", and "beloved" and nouns such as "delight", "joy" and "darling" a contrast to the sinister descriptions of previous stanzas. Although he has not met the grown-up Maud, some of the language is already potentially erotic. She has a "sweet purse-mouth when my father dangled the grapes", and was a "moon-faced darling of all". Future sections (such as parts 2 and 3) fixate upon Maud's face and mouth. Stanza 18 ends with a long dash, as if the narrator is keen to continue fantasizing about Maud's beauty.

However, stanza 19 cuts these pleasant thoughts off, as the narrator snaps out of the pleasant memories with a series of short, abrupt clauses: "What is she now? My dreams are bad. She may bring me a curse". Again, the use of a three part line serves to break up the normal hexameter rhythm, to signal the agitation of the narrator. The narrator then uses a metaphor of hunting, saying there is "fatter game on the moor". This means there is a more tempting prey for the hunter, and here it means that the narrator realizes he is not a good marriage match for Maud and her father. It also sees marriage in terms of hunting and value, which is very mercenary, but in keeping with the brutal realities of the time. The narrator then turns in on himself and says he will remain isolated. Again he uses an image of death and burial, saying that "I will bury myself in myself", which means he will be solitary and not reach out to others. This also foreshadows the terrible scenes in the foreign asylum in part two, when he imagines himself dead, buried, and speaking from underneath the earth itself.

Stanza 19 alludes twice to the Devil. Firstly, the narrator uses a strange saying "for the fiend best knows whether woman or man be the worse"; this seems to show a deep mistrust of women. The next saying ends the stanza: "the Devil may pipe to his own". This phrase seems to imply that Maud might be evil, like her father – that she may bring the "curse" the narrator mentions in the first line of the stanza (which also echoes stanza 6, in which the female figure of Peace brought a curse). These phrases appear very colloquial, like old proverbs, and are not very "poetic", as was remarked upon by critics of Tennyson's own times. The narrator is making himself deliberately unpleasant in these ugly proverbs, shutting himself off from others, and brooding on thoughts of evil and the Devil.

II

LONG have I sigh'd for a calm: God grant I may find it at last!
It will never be broken by Maud, she has neither savour nor salt,
But a cold and clear-cut face, as I found when her carriage past,
Perfectly beautiful: let it be granted her: where is the fault?          *80*
All that I saw (for her eyes were downcast, not to be seen)
Faultily faultless, icily regular, splendidly null,
Dead perfection, no more; nothing more, if it had not been
For a chance of travel, a paleness, an hour's defect of the rose,
Or an underlip, you may call it a little too ripe, too full,          *85*
Or the least little delicate aquiline curve in a sensitive nose,
From which I escaped heart-free, with the least little touch of spleen.

Synopsis

Part two opens after the narrator has seen Maud's face as she passed in a carriage; she has returned from abroad. Although he tries to convince himself that he is not interested in her, claiming to find her appearance cold and unattractive, his obsession with describing her face betrays the fact he is already beginning to fall in love with her.

Verse form

Part two is a single long stanza, with 11 lines. Each line is, as in part one, a hexameter with six stresses, often divided into two "hemistichs" or halves by a central pause or "caesura". The first four lines rhyme ABAB, the form of part one, but lines 5 to 11 rhyme ABACBCA, which prepares us for the greater freedom in verse form that Tennyson uses throughout the rest of the poem, to express the ebbs and flows of the narrator's love for Maud.

Stanza 1

The first two lines are very regular in their metre, with a strong central pause. As in part one, such regular metre usually means the narrator is trying to be rational about his emotions, and here we see the same theme; he has for a long time tried to be "calm", and turns to God to pray for it. Line two shows the narrator being resolute, telling us his calm "will never be broken by Maud", as she has "neither savour nor salt". This metaphor, taken from cooking, means she is insipid, bland and tasteless. She has a "cold and clear-cut face", which he glimpsed from a carriage that past the narrator on the road. The hard "c" sounds emphasize the narrator's view that Maud seems cold and distant, but also the fact that he is trying to harden his heart against her.

However, we get a sense that the narrator is trying to bottle up his emotions in lines four and six of this stanza, where the line splits into three parts – as we have seen, usually a sign of strong emotion. In line 4, the narrator admits, grudgingly, that Maud is "Perfectly beautiful: let it be granted her: where is the fault", almost as if he is looking for a fault to justify rejecting his feelings for her. The colons in this line make the pauses seem very abrupt indeed. Although he saw her only briefly and did not ever see her eyes, he continues in line 6 to criticize her. She is "Faultily faultless, icily regular, splendidly null". The first part of this is an oxymoron, or a contradiction in terms: how can someone be "faultily faultless" – as if her very perfection was a problem? The narrator seems here to be making little sense, which should alert us to the fact he might have growing feelings for Maud. The final phrase, "splendidly null" is an unpleasant way of saying she is worthless, in spite of appearing so perfect, again an odd way of criticizing someone, and which alerts to us deeper, hidden emotions in the narrator.

The next line continues in the same way, with Maud described as "Dead perfection, no more". As throughout the length of the poem, death is never very far from the surface, and this word appearing stressed at the start of a line foreshadows Maud's own fate.

However, at this point in part two, the narrator's true feelings break out in a series of descriptions of her face which focus on tiny details, and signal that in glimpsing her in the carriage, he noticed everything about her. She is not "faultily faultless" but instead has a number of highly distinctive features. She was pale from travel, which the narrator describes as "an hour's defect of the rose". This introduces a key symbol for Maud throughout the poem – the red rose, which symbolizes desire, blood, and ultimately death. After the "sweet-purse mouth" he remembered in part 1, the narrator again fixates on her mouth in the next line, when he notices the supposed defect of "an underlip, you may call it a little too ripe, too full". In using "ripe", usually used for fruit, Tennyson is creating a very erotic image, which carries within it a foreshadowing of the physical passion between the narrator and Maud.

The narrator then moves to describe the rest of her face, which has a "delicate little aquiline curve in a sensitive nose". Aquiline comes from the Latin for like an eagle, and means curved like a beak. This is another description that is actually attractive, not a defect. Part two ends with the narrator deluding himself by stating that he escaped from these sights "heart-free, with the least little touch of spleen". The word "spleen" relates to an old theory of emotion, in which the body was affected by fluids or "humours". The word could mean angry – in modern English, "splenetic" comes from the same root. However, it could also mean sad or melancholy, which is how it was used in a set of very famous poems in mid-19th century France, by Charles Baudelaire: *Les Fleurs du Mal*. The fact "spleen" could mean either angry or sad shows how the narrator is divided in his emotions towards Maud, and does not truly understand his own reaction to her. He has certainly not escaped "heart-free", as part 3 makes clear.

## III

COLD and clear-cut face, why come you so cruelly meek,
Breaking a slumber in which all spleenful folly was drown'd,
Pale with the golden beam of an eyelash dead on the cheek,     *90*
Passionless, pale, cold face, star-sweet on a gloom profound;
Womanlike, taking revenge too deep for a transient wrong
Done but in thought to your beauty, and ever as pale as before
Growing and fading and growing upon me without a sound,
Luminous, gemlike, ghostlike, deathlike, half the night long     *95*
Growing and fading and growing, till I could bear it no more,
But arose, and all by myself in my own dark garden ground,
Listening now to the tide in its broad-flung ship-wrecking roar,
Now to the scream of a madden'd beach dragg'd down by the wave,
Walk'd in a wintry wind by a ghastly glimmer, and found     *100*
The shining daffodil dead, and Orion low in his grave.

Synopsis

Part three follows on from two; the narrator has been kept awake all night by visions of Maud's face, in spite of his claims that he was not moved by seeing her. Unable to sleep, he rises and walks round his garden, describing the natural world in increasingly more agitated ways.

Verse form

The whole of part three is fourteen lines long, again in loosely structured hexameters. A common verse form in fourteen lines is a sonnet, but that has a more rigid verse form than part three. Again, the first four lines rhyme ABAB, before different rhymes are introduced, the whole form being tied together by the B rhyme repeating 5 times throughout the whole piece (drown'd, profound, sound, ground, found). This clever mix of variation and repetition in the rhyme is a characteristic of Tennyson's use of verse in *Maud*, showing the battle between reason and passion in the narrator.

Stanza 1

This opens with a repetition of the third line of part two, "Cold and clear-cut face", but this time the narrator is much more tortured and anguished. He addresses this vision of Maud's face directly: "why come you so cruelly meek", appearing so gentle and calm, but ruining his calm, a "slumber in which all spleenful folly was drown'd". The word "spleenful" again echoes part two, meaning the emotion provoked by seeing Maud, a mixture of sadness and anger. The morbid echo of death in "drown'd" returns in the description of the vision of Maud's face "Pale with the golden beam of an eyelash dead on the cheek"; the word "dead" once more foreshadows Maud's death.

The narrator continues in the next line to use a series of unexpected adjectives to describe his vision. Maud's face is "Passionless, pale, cold", repeating his previous description, but he uses a compound adjective in an odd phrase that emphasizes Maud's own melancholy expression, "star-sweet on a gloom profound". "The word "star-sweet" is strange as stars are not normally described as sweet – at this point he is beginning to change, perhaps, from the view of Maud as remote, cold and unattainable, to the language he used to talk about her as a child, with a "sweet purse-mouth".

The next sentence is also difficult: "Womanlike, taking revenge too deep for a transient wrong / Done but in thought to your beauty". He implies that the vision is tormenting him because he has done some wrong to Maud. This seems to point to the narrator having indulged in a sexual fantasy about Maud. There is a sense of guilt here, in that the narrator has stepped over the bounds he imposed in his future relationship to Maud.

Lines 94-96 describe with increasing horror the vision of Maud's face. The phrase "Growing and fading and growing" is repeated, stressing the inescapable nature of the nightmare. The face is "gemlike, ghostlike, deathlike", three similes which let us know how beautiful, but how horrifying the image is. Again, we see death intrude as a key theme of the poem, and here death is linked explicitly with Maud's face.

The narrator can take this no longer, and rises to walk around his own "garden ground". The repeated "g" sounds echo the "growing and fading" and "ghostlike", and are picked up a couple of lines later in "ghastly glimmer"; this technique lets us know there is no respite for the narrator from his nightmare in the outside world. The narrator listens to the sea, which is not calming but has a "broad-flung ship-wrecking roar", two compound adjectives created by Tennyson here to emphasize the narrator's distress. This use of the pathetic fallacy – when nature echoes a character's feelings – continues in the description of the "scream of a madden'd beach". We can also see an echo of the description in part one of the narrator's father, driven mad by being cheated, who "walk'd when the wind like a broken worldling wail'd (part one, line 11). Here the same "w" sound mimics the sound of the wind, as the narrator "Walk'd in a wintry wind by a ghastly glimmer". The son and the father have the same experience.

Two more disturbing images close this scene. The "shining daffodil dead" introduces death again (the daffodil is usually a symbol of joy, as in William Wordsworth's 1815 celebrated poem *Daffodils*). Secondly, a group of stars moving below the horizon is described as "Orion low in his grave". (Orion the Hunter, a figure from Greek myth, is the name of a constellation). By mentioning "grave" here, we again see the narrator's ability to see death everywhere.

# IV

## 1

A MILLION emeralds break from the ruby-budded lime
In the little grove where I sit—ah, wherefore cannot I be
Like things of the season gay, like the bountiful season bland,
When the far-off sail is blown by the breeze of a softer clime,    *105*
Half-lost in the liquid azure bloom of a crescent of sea,
The silent sapphire-spangled marriage ring of the land?

## 2

Below me, there, is the village, and looks how quiet and small!
And yet bubbles o'er like a city, with gossip, scandal, and spite;
And Jack on his ale-house bench has as many lies as a Czar;    *110*
And here on the landward side, by a red rock, glimmers the Hall;
And up in the high Hall-garden I see her pass like a light;
But sorrow seize me if ever that light be my leading star!

## 3

When have I bow'd to her father, the wrinkled head of the race?
I met her to-day with her brother, but not to her brother I bow'd;    *115*
I bow'd to his lady-sister as she rode by on the moor;
But the fire of a foolish pride flash'd over her beautiful face.
O child, you wrong your beauty, believe it, in being so proud;
Your father has wealth well-gotten, and I am nameless and poor.

## 4    *120*

I keep but a man and a maid, ever ready to slander and steal;
I know it, and smile a hard-set smile, like a stoic, or like
A wiser epicurean, and let the world have its way:
For nature is one with rapine, a harm no preacher can heal;
The Mayfly is torn by the swallow, the sparrow spear'd by the shrike,
And the whole little wood where I sit is a world of plunder and prey.    *125*

Synopsis

The narrator sits in his garden contemplating the beauty of the view of the sea, and wishing he could be as happy as the scene implies. However, this wistful mood does not last. He turns inland to the village, and sees only the same faults as in a big city. Looking at the Hall reminds him he saw Maud and her brother out recently, and he notes that she appeared full of pride. The narrator's view of nature then sours, and he describes it as brutal and vicious.

Verse form

Again, Tennyson in part four uses hexameters. There is a regular rhyme scheme through all ten stanzas in part 4: ABCABC, which makes this one of the most regular sections of the whole poem, as the theme is often quite cold, distant and analytical, in spite of moments of emotional outburst.

Stanza 1 to 4

Stanza 1 opens with an extremely poetic use of hyperbole or overstatement, as a vivid metaphor describes the effect of light coming through the lime-tree branches. It is like "A million emeralds", the buds resembling the green gems, sparkling. The use of the word "ah" though, is onomatopoeia, as it represents a sigh, the narrator saddened that he cannot be happy, unlike the world around him. The vocabulary is very positive, the weather "bountiful and bland", unlike the "wintry wind" of the previous section. Here there is merely "the breeze of a softer clime" which does not wreck boats, but gently fills their sails. The sea is not violent, as it was in section three, but a "liquid azure bloom", a metaphor cleverly linking the garden in which he sits with the sea. The final metaphor in the stanza imagines the sea circling the land like a "silent sapphire-spangled marriage ring". The use of a wedding ring shows the narrator's hopes he will one day marry Maud, as well as being a symbol of cosmic harmony.

However, stanza 2 breaks this spell; we remember that the narrator cannot, in his agitated state, "be / Like things of the season gay" (gay here meaning happy or beautiful). He looks down on the village and sees only its faults. The place "bubbles o'er like a city with gossip, scandal and spite". The word "bubbles" is a metaphor taken from boiling water, and means that there is an uncontrollable amount of the worst side of human nature below.

The narrator cleverly introduces a brief portrait of a villager, comparing him with the Czar, or Emperor of Russia: "Jack on his ale-house bench has as many lies as a Czar". Czar Nicholas I of Russia at this time was threatening British interests, especially in the collapsing Ottoman Empire (modern Turkey), and there was much criticism of the Czar's aggression. Eventually this would lead to the Crimean War, in which the narrator plans to enlist in part 3. (*Maud* was published in 1855, and the Crimean War ran from 1853 to 1856. One of *Maud*'s most famous companion poems, *The Charge of the Light Brigade*, was about a disastrous battle during this conflict.) Alluding to the Czar's "lies" makes the poem very topical and engaged with wider politics. After this political allusion, the narrator focuses back on the Hall, and Maud herself. He has seen her pass "like a light", a simile stressing her ability to illuminate the narrator's sad life, though he vows that "sorrow seize me if ever that light be my leading star!" This metaphor – from navigation, meaning using the stars to steer a ship – is in keeping with the ship imagery of earlier stanzas, and means the narrator fears being ruined by Maud, like a ship can be wrecked on the rocks.

Stanza three recalls the meeting between Maud, her brother, and the narrator. The narrator tells us he did not bow to Maud's father, or her brother, only to her. He was met however by an expression he reads as pride, the intensity of his distress signaled in the repeated alliteration of the "f" sounds in "the fire of a foolish pride flash;d over her beautiful face". He criticizes her for being so proud, as her father "has wealth well gotten, and I am nameless and poor". The word "well-gotten" is unusual, and meant ironically; the normal phrase is "ill-gotten", which means obtained by deceit. We know that Maud's father has ill-gotten gains, having swindled the narrator's father.

The narrator becomes increasingly bitter. He only has unreliable servants, ready to steal from him. He tries to bear this like philosophers in Ancient Greece, either as a "stoic" or believer in the need to accept trouble calmly, or an "epicurean", follower of Epicurus and his belief in a world without morals and only physical pleasures. Nature is no longer "bland" but "one with rapine", which means violent theft. He can only see the way that creatures kill each other, such as a "sparrow spear'd by the shrike", a small, sharp-beaked bird. The harsh sibilance of "s" sounds emphasizes his horror that his precious wood is really a "world of plunder and prey".

5

We are puppets, Man in his pride, and Beauty fair in her flower;
Do we move ourselves, or are we moved by an unseen hand at a game
That pushes us off from the board, and others ever succeed?
Ah yet, we cannot be kind to each other here for an hour;
We whisper, and hint, and chuckle, and grin at a brother's shame;    *130*
However we brave it out, we men are a little breed.

6

A monstrous eft was of old the Lord and Master of Earth,
For him did his high sun flame, and his river billowing ran,
And he felt himself in his force to be Nature's crowning race.
As nine months go to the shaping an infant ripe for his birth,    *135*
So many a million of ages have gone to the making of man:
He now is first, but is he the last? is he not too base?

7

The man of science himself is fonder of glory, and vain,
An eye well-practised in nature, a spirit bounded and poor;
The passionate heart of the poet is whirl'd into folly and vice.    *140*
I would not marvel at either, but keep a temperate brain;
For not to desire or admire, if a man could learn it, were more
Than to walk all day like the sultan of old in a garden of spice.

8

For the drift of the Maker is dark, an Isis hid by the veil.
Who knows the ways of the world, how God will bring them about?    *145*
Our planet is one, the suns are many, the world is wide.
Shall I weep if a Poland fall? shall I shriek if a Hungary fail?
Or an infant civilisation be ruled with rod or with knout?
I have not made the world, and He that made it will guide.

Synopsis

Stanzas 5 to 8 are mainly concerned with philosophy and science, and the lowly position of humanity in the universe in an age of rapid scientific discovery. Human beings are likened to puppets, and playthings of fate. The narrator talks about recent theories of evolution, to compare current people to the age of the dinosaurs, and he implies that humankind will one day disappear as well. Both science and poetry are criticized as useless. The narrator believes it is better to avoid all pity for others, and give in to the will of God.

Stanzas 5 – 8

Two metaphors dominate stanza five. People are firstly compared to puppets; this means that, like marionettes moved by strings, they are not in control of themselves. Men are ruled instead by their "pride" and women with their "Beauty" or vanity. The second metaphor likens people to chess pieces, and the narrator asks whether "we are moved by an unseen hand at a game / That pushes us off from the board, and others ever succeed?" The board here means life, and some die or fail, and others are successful. These images reflect the way the narrator feels out of control in his life, which has been dominated by the actions of others (the Lord of the Manor), or by his own emotions. The stanza ends with the narrator using a powerful series of verbs to describe how people treat each other badly; "whisper", "hint", "chuckle", and "grin". The final line is very calm and balanced, with a strong central pause or caesura, to make the statement very clear: "However we brave it out, we men are a little breed".

The sixth stanza mentions new theories of geology and evolution, which were being discussed in the early 19th century. Although Charles Darwin published his *On the Origin of Species* in 1858, after *Maud* was written, geologists had already argued since the late 18th century that the world was millions of years old. The Bible had before this said the world was only 6,000 years old. Fossils represented lost creatures, and humans were only part of this story, and may not always be the dominant species. Tennyson has the narrator use these arguments to show that human beings are not as powerful as they think they are. Stanza six introduces the idea that a "monstrous eft", or huge lizard or dinosaur, was once "Lord and Master of Earth". The narrator imagines the feelings of the dinosaur, reveling in his power, over nature: "For him did his high sun flame, and his river billowing ran". The dinosaur felt himself "Nature's crowning race". The next two lines compare the nine months pregnancy of a single human being to the vast amounts of time it took to create humanity. The narrator then leaves these thoughts open-ended, as a rhetorical question returns to the theme of stanza five. In time other creatures might replace humanity, as our nature is too "base" or weak to continue: "He now is first, but is he the last? is he not too base?" The view of nature here is of life as a battle or race, which is in keeping with the narrator's view of the nobility of war.

Stanza seven contrasts "the man of science" to the "passionate heart of the poet", but neither seems to have any positive qualities. The scientist is too fond of "glory" and "vain", with a "spirit bounded and poor". This means they are lacking in imagination. The poet, whilst imaginative, is "whirl'd into folly and vice", a metaphor taken from agitated or violent movement, which means they lack stability or calm good sense. The narrator wishes to steer a middle way, and keep a "temperate brain". It would be better "not to desire or admire", but keep away from strong emotions at all. The narrator uses an image taken from stories of the Orient, popularized in books such as the recent 1840 translation (by Edward Lane) of the Arabian *One Thousand and One Nights* (or *Arabian Nights*). It would be better to avoid all strong emotion than "to walk all day like the sultan of old in a garden of spice". The sultan is an Arabic word for ruler. This line is very beautiful, however, the rhythm divided into three parts instead of two, which usually signals that the narrator is showing a strong emotional reaction. Tennyson does this to show that the narrator perhaps does not really believe what he is saying here.

Stanza eight, after the brief moment of calm in the garden, returns the narrator's increasingly dark view of the world. The narrator acknowledges the darkness, telling us that the "drift of the maker is dark", or that God's meaning or "drift" is inexplicable. God's plan is an "Isis hid by the veil", Isis here meaning the goddess of Ancient Egypt. This image implies that ancient religion and Christianity are both equally obscure, which is a daring view for the 19th century. The narrator then hardens his heart against tragic events, which are petty seen on a cosmic scale, as "the suns are many, the world is wide". He alludes to Poland and Hungary in Eastern Europe, who were struggling for independence (both had recent failed revolutions in 1848), and asks why he should "weep" over any country ruled through tyranny, by "rod or with knout" (or whip). He seems resigned to letting evil triumph, claiming it is God's will: "I have not made the world, and He that made it will guide."

## 9

Be mine a philosopher's life in the quiet woodland ways,
Where if I cannot be gay let a passionless peace be my lot,
Far-off from the clamour of liars belied in the hubbub of lies;
From the long-neck'd geese of the world that are ever hissing dispraise
Because their natures are little, and, whether he heed it or not,
Where each man walks with his head in a cloud of poisonous flies.

## 10

And most of all would I flee from the cruel madness of love,
The honey of poison-flowers and all the measureless ill.
Ah Maud, you milkwhite fawn, you are all unmeet for a wife.
Your mother is mute in her grave as her image in marble above;
Your father is ever in London, you wander about at your will;
You have but fed on the roses, and lain in the lilies of life.

Synopsis

Stanzas 9-10 complete section 4. The narrator continues to long for a quiet life, free from what he calls the "cruel madness" of love. He ends the section by saying that Maud is not a suitable wife for him.

Stanzas 9 -10

The narrator opens Stanza nine by claiming he wishes to lead a "philosopher's life", and hide away from the world. If he cannot be happy, he wishes to live in a "passionless peace". This is ironic, as in previous sections he criticized peace as being a danger to the happiness of England. He uses two metaphors in the Stanza drawn from nature to talk about the people he would like to avoid. Firstly, he wants to stay away from the "long-neck'd geese of the world that are ever hissing dispraise". He compares people to geese, who are noisy and aggressive; this shows his distrust of people who constantly criticize others. The word "hissing" is an example of onomatopoeia, and sounds like a goose's cry, and means that what they say is unpleasant. The next metaphor is even more horrible. He talks about people whose natures are "little" or small-minded, and says that "each man walks with his head in a cloud of poisonous flies". The cloud of poisonous flies is a metaphor which represents the unpleasant thoughts that surround everyone, which mean that they cannot see things clearly. A cloud of flies also signifies that something is decaying, which picks up the theme of death.

Stanza 10 finally expresses what the narrator is most afraid of: the "cruel madness of love". Again, the narrator uses images of the natural world in a very negative way. He uses the phrase the "honey of poison-flowers" to refer to Maud. This means that what is beautiful and sweet might actually cause harm. In the third line of the Stanza, he addresses Maud directly by name, and calls her a "milkwhite faun". A faun is a young deer; he describes her in this way to emphasize her youth, beauty and her innocence, but he then follows this with a very clear statement that she is unsuitable for him: "you are all unmeet for a wife".

The narrator explains why she is unsuitable. Maud's mother is dead and her father absent, which means she has been allowed to do as she wants, and has not had to grow up. The final line has an image of two flowers, which will be very symbolic throughout the rest of the poem: "You have but fed on the roses, and lain in the lilies of life". To feed on the roses means that she has only ever had good luck. The meaning here is that Maud has had no experience of what is bad, only what is good, unlike the narrator, who has suffered due to his father's fate. Roses, as noted earlier, usually mean passion or desire, which is contrasted to lilies, which are one of the images used for the Virgin Mary, and symbolize purity.

The narrator is therefore again unable to decide whether he should love Maud, or whether he should leave her alone.

# V

## 1

A VOICE by the cedar tree,
In the meadow under the Hall!
She is singing an air that is known to me,
A passionate ballad gallant and gay,                    *165*
A martial song like a trumpet's call!
Singing alone in the morning of life,
In the happy morning of life and of May,
Singing of men that in battle array,
Ready in heart and ready in hand,                       *170*
March with banner and bugle and fife
To the death, for their native land.

## 2

Maud with her exquisite face,
And wild voice pealing up to the sunny sky,
And feet like sunny gems on an English green,          *175*
Maud in the light of her youth and her grace,
Singing of Death, and of Honour that cannot die,
Till I well could weep for a time so sordid and mean,
And myself so languid and base.

## 3                                                    *180*

Silence, beautiful voice!
Be still, for you only trouble the mind
With a joy in which I cannot rejoice,
A glory I shall not find.
Still! I will hear you no more,                         *185*
For your sweetness hardly leaves me a choice
But to move to the meadow and fall before
Her feet on the meadow grass, and adore,
Not her, who is neither courtly nor kind
Not her, not her, but a voice.

Synopsis

Part five is a short section, in which the (hidden) narrator overhears Maud singing a ballad (or popular song) about soldiers going to war. The narrator is deeply moved by Maud's voice and theme of the song, and wishes he could join in and go to battle, rather than continue to suffer from his own depression and lack of activity.

Verse Form

Tennyson abandons hexameters for three irregular Stanzas of mainly short lines, which are more like the lyrics of a song. This reflects the content of the section, as the narrator overhears Maud singing.

Stanzas 1-3

The first stanza does not mention Maud by name. The narrator hears "A voice by the cedar tree / In the meadow under the Hall!" The voice is singing a song familiar to the narrator, a "passionate ballad gallant and gay". The alliteration of the "g" sounds here shows how the song is pleasant to the ear. A ballad is a popular form of music, and many ballads have themes of love and war, the very themes of *Maud* itself. The music is "like a trumpet's call" to the narrator. It is a "martial song", which means this particular song has a theme of battle and war.

Maud is "Singing alone in the morning of life". The phrase "morning of life" means she is very young. The first rhyming couplet in the whole poem comes here, which again shows how the verse forms in this section are more musical than the previous four sections. The phrase "morning of life" is repeated, adding to the effect: Maud is "In the happy morning of life and of May / Singing of men that in battle array" are off to war. The men, though, are off to their death, which comes as a shock after these uplifting lines. The men march "with banner and bugle and fife / To the death, for their native land". A "fife" is a small flute, and a bugle a small trumpet. The music is glorifying war. The alliteration of the "b" sounds in "banner" and "bugle" echoes the sound of marching feet.

The second stanza is much shorter. As in previous sections, the narrator is obsessed by Maud's face, here described as "exquisite" or very beautiful. Her "wild voice" is "pealing", which is a metaphor taken from the sound of bells, and means her voice is clear, and very strong. The narrator uses a simile in line three, describing her feet as "like sunny gems on an English green". This means her feet shine in the sun, as she walks barefoot on the grass, and shows how beautiful the narrator finds her. The narrator uses a technique called juxtaposition here to contrast this beautiful scene with the violent lyrics of her song. While Maud is in "the light of her youth" she is nevertheless "Singing of Death, and of Honour that cannot die". Again, this shows the narrator sees war as being glorious.

Stanza two ends with the narrator weeping at the song. This line is twelve syllables long, the longest in the whole section, which contrasts with the short lines of the first stanza. The unexpected length of this line shows how the narrator is caught up in his own emotion, not in the sounds of the song: "Till I well myself could weep for a time so sordid and mean". We are back in the themes of section four, and the narrator's view that modern life is unpleasant and meaningless, and he himself is unworthy: "myself so languid and base". Languid means slow and lazy here, in contrast with the active sacrifice of the soldiers.

In contrast with the long line in stanza two, the third stanza opens with the shortest line in the section, at only six syllables: "Silence, beautiful voice!" which implies a pause after it, as if Maud has fallen silent. The narrator returns to the theme that Maud disturbs his attempts to find peace. She can "only trouble the mind / With a joy in which I cannot rejoice". The echo of "joy" in "rejoice" sounds harsh, and seems like a "tautology" or needless repetition, which shows the narrator is disturbed. Maud's song talks of a "glory" which the narrator cannot share.

Tennyson here use the technique of enjambment to show the narrator's growing emotion, breaking a sentence over a number of line endings. The narrator commands Maud to be quiet, as if he continues to listen, he will have no choice but to "fall before / Her feet on the meadow grass, and adore / Not her, who is neither courtly nor kind / Not her, not her, but a voice". This very complicated line simply means that if he stays and listens to her song he will fall in love with an idealized vision of Maud, not the real Maud who is cruel (he already thinks she has acted in a haughty manner with him). Ending this difficult section with the words "a voice" – which also opened the first stanza – is very musical, like a piece of music which opens and closes with the same phrase, and shows Tennyson's skill in creating a sense of structure and order, even in the middle of the narrator's most disturbed emotions.

# VI

## 1

MORNING arises stormy and pale,
No sun, but a wannish glare
In fold upon fold of hueless cloud,
And the budded peaks of the wood are bow'd
Caught and cuff'd by the gale:
I had fancied it would be fair.

## 2

Whom but Maud should I meet
Last night, when the sunset burn'd
On the blossom'd gable-ends
At the head of the village street,
Whom but Maud should I meet?
And she touch'd my hand with a smile so sweet
She made me divine amends
For a courtesy not return'd.

## 3

And thus a delicate spark
Of glowing and growing light
Thro' the livelong hours of the dark
Kept itself warm in the heart of my dreams,
Ready to burst in a colour'd flame;
Till at last when the morning came
In a cloud, it faded, and seems
But an ashen-gray delight.

## 4

What if with her sunny hair,
And smile as sunny as cold,
She meant to weave me a snare
Of some coquettish deceit,
Cleopatra-like as of old
To entangle me when we met,
To have her lion roll in a silken net
And fawn at a victor's feet.

Synopsis

In part six the narrator recounts meeting Maud, who is friendly towards him, reawakening his interest in her. However, the narrator cannot decide whether she is as kind as she appears, or is simply acting like this to deceive and entrap him, or get him to support her brother in the upcoming elections.

Verse Form

As in part five, Tennyson uses stanzas of different lengths, with short lines, giving an energetic, lyric quality to the verse. The stanzas are between six and seventeen lines long, and the longest stanzas (six and eight) contain the most agitated verse, the length of the stanza increasing with the narrator's obsession and unhappiness.

Stanzas 1-4

The first stanza uses the pathetic fallacy – with nature echoing the narrator's mood. The morning is "stormy and pale", with no sun and endless cloud. In line four, the harsh alliteration of "c" sounds show how the trees are violently "Caught and cuff'd by the gale". The word "cuff'd" means hit, as a person might be hit in the face. This shows how the narrator too feels violently affected by his emotions. The last line shows the narrator's disappointment: "I had fancied it would be fair". This echoes his disappointment with Maud, that he cannot control his emotions.

In stanza two, we learn that the narrator, for the first time, met Maud the previous evening, in a scene characterized by beautiful weather, which raised the narrator's spirits. He uses imagery of fire to express his feelings, and the difference from the pale and colourless morning. He met "when the sunset burn'd / On the blossom'd gable-ends", which is a very beautiful image, and again a use of the pathetic fallacy, nature mirroring the narrator's happiness. He repeats in lines one and five the same phrase, "Whom but Maud should I meet", to express his surprise, and we see that Maud has made "divine amends / For a courtesy not return'd" – which means she has treated him very kindly this time. The "smile so sweet" phrase will occur again through part six, forming a sort of chorus or refrain, as the narrator alternates between distrust of Maud, and a growing feeling of love for her. The use of the word "divine", which normal relates to God, here shows the depth of the narrator's feelings.

Stanza three develops the metaphor of fire. Like a "delicate spark" the narrator's love for Maud "kept itself warm in the heart of my dreams / Ready to burst in a colour'd flame". This images means that meeting Maud, though only a small incident, like a spark could smoulder unseen all night but burst into a greater fire at a future date. It means that his emotions could grow from this meeting to have a greater importance. The internal rhyme of "glowing and growing light" emphasizes how overwhelming the narrator's feelings for Maud could become. However, we are suddenly taken back to the atmosphere of the first stanza, with the grey morning weather showing how quickly the narrator's hopes can be dashed. The "delicate spark" of his love has faded in the clouds to an "ashen-grey delight". This means that the fire of the narrator's love has gone out. This is represented in the grey morning, which is like the grey ashes left after the fire.

The next stanza illustrates why the narrator is unable to sustain his love for Maud; he does not trust her, and tortures himself that she is out to deceive him. The images used are misogynistic (or woman-hating), and show the narrator's distrust of women and female sexuality. He first uses a metaphor from hunting; the narrator asks himself whether her "sunny hair" and "smile" would weave a "snare / Of some coquettish deceit". A snare is type of trap used by hunters; the word "coquettish" means someone who acts in a flirtatious manner to attract a person. This means therefore Maud might be showing affection to trap the narrator into falling for her.

The narrator then alludes to Cleopatra (69-30 BCE), who was Queen of Ancient Egypt. She had a famous love affair with the Roman Emperor Julius Caesar, and also after his death with his General and friend Mark Anthony. In Shakespeare's play *Anthony and Cleopatra* (c 1607) the ageing Mark Anthony is shown as being weakened by his love for Cleopatra. In *Maud*, in a very similar way, the narrator uses a metaphor of losing masculine power, and being dominated by Maud's sexuality. The narrator risks being captured and emasculated (or made to appear unmanly): "To have her lion roll in a silken net / And fawn at a victor's feet". A lion is the ultimate symbol of male power and pride – they are known as the "king of the jungle", and to be caught in a "silken net" means this power her been taken away by female beauty. To "fawn" means to show slavish devotion – another unmanly image.

Ah, what shall I be at fifty
Should Nature keep me alive,
If I find the world so bitter
When I am but twenty-five?
Yet, if she were not a cheat,
If Maud were all that she seem'd,
And her smile were all that I dream'd,
Then the world were not so bitter
But a smile could make it sweet.

6

What if tho' her eye seem'd full
Of a kind intent to me,
What if that dandy-despot, he,
That jewell'd mass of millinery,
That oil'd and curl'd Assyrian Bull
Smelling of musk and of insolence,
Her brother, from whom I keep aloof,
Who wants the finer politic sense
To mask, tho' but in his own behoof,
With a glassy smile his brutal scorn—
What if he had told her yestermorn
How prettily for his own sweet sake
A face of tenderness might be feign'd,
And a moist mirage in desert eyes,
That so, when the rotten hustings shake
In another month to his brazen lies,
A wretched vote may be gain'd.

7

For a raven ever croaks, at my side,
Keep watch and ward, keep watch and ward,
Or thou wilt prove their tool.
Yea too, myself from myself I guard,
For often a man's own angry pride
Is cap and bells for a fool.

Synopsis

Stanzas five to seven show the narrator again alternating between hope that Maud is genuine, and fear she is deceiving him to further her brother's political ambitions. Stanza six is a lengthy description of the brother in very extravagant language, and stanza seven shows the narrator trying to be wary of his own emotions and love for Maud.

Stanzas 5 -7

Stanza five shows the narrator fearful that he is becoming "bitter" or losing hope with the world. He is only twenty-five years old, and he fears that when he is fifty, he will be even more disillusioned. Tennyson cleverly shows how the narrator is unhappy and out of step with the world by the fact that there is no rhyme-word for the word "fifty" which ends line one; instead line three unexpectedly ends with the word "bitter", which is harsh on the ear and shows the narrator's lack of ease. The word "fifty" is the only unrhymed line-ending in the poem to date. The stanza concludes, typically, with the narrator returning to the image of Maud's smile as sweet; if she were genuine, the bitterness he feels would be changed: "the world were not so bitter / But a smile could make it sweet".

Stanza six, though, typically for this section, does not allow the narrator any time to dwell upon Maud's positive influence, as a seventeen line stanza grows increasingly obsessed by Maud's brother and his bad influence on Maud. Tennyson uses very exotic imagery to show the obsession that the narrator has with the brother; such exotic imagery is used to make the brother seem ridiculous.

Firstly, the narrator stresses the brother's extravagant clothes, which show how superficial and vain he is. The brother is a "dandy-despot", which means a tyrant, but dressed in a very showy manner. He is a "jewell'd mass of millinery". This means he is obsessed by clothes and is a frivolous and shallow character. The alliteration of "d" and "m" sounds show how agitated the narrator is becoming. Secondly, the narrator moves on to the personal appearance of the brother. He is an "oil'd and curl'd Assyrian Bull / Smelling of musk and insolence". This is a very strange image, and focuses upon the excessive care the brother takes of his hair, and the perfumes (or "musk") that he wears. The narrator then tries to belittle the brother by comparing him to a bull, a large and aggressive animal, implying that the brother is like an animal, not a person, and therefore stupid. The word "insolence" here also betrays the fact that the brother is not giving the narrator the respect the narrator thinks he deserves. The word "Assyrian" means from the Middle East. The narrator is using this in a racist way, as describing the brother as foreign this makes him less English and therefore less admirable in the narrator's eyes.

The rest of the stanza shows the narrator anxious that the brother might have told Maud how to pretend to be nice. Although the brother is too stupid to be able to hide his own "brutal scorn", Maud is more intelligent. The narrator uses a metaphor from geography here. The brother might, in the narrator's paranoia, have told Maud "How prettily for his own sweet sake / A face of tenderness might be feign'd / And a moist mirage in desert eyes". A mirage is an optical illusion of a lake or body of water seen by traveler in a desert; it is an illusion caused by heat haze. Here, it means that the tears that came to Maud's eyes yesterday are false, as a mirage is. It is a striking and powerful image. The tears would have manipulated the narrator so that when there is a "rotten hustings" or corrupt election next month, the narrator would vote for Maud's brother to be a Member of Parliament (or MP).

Stanza seven opens with a strange image – a raven "ever croaks" at the narrator's side. The word "croaks" here is an example of onomatopoeia, and the next line also imagines the raven's voice, but it seems to repeat an English phrase, "keep watch and ward". This phrase means be careful, or the narrator might prove the "tool" of Maud and her brother, or used for their ends. Again, the natural world echoes the narrator's feelings. (The raven was associated with the supernatural in 19th century literature – as in Edgar Allen Poe's poem *The Raven* [1845]. The Raven is sometimes a bringer of bad luck, but in Ancient Greece was a messenger of Apollo and provided help and advice. In Poe's poem, a talking Raven also appears, and a young man descends into madness over his love for a beautiful woman Lenore, a narrative that resembles *Maud*).

The stanza ends with the narrator using a metaphor drawn from the medieval royal court; he realizes that his "angry pride" could be "cap and bells for a fool". A fool or court jester wore cap and bells to signal his lowly position; here the narrator means that he needs to beware of his own emotions; when he says "myself from myself I guard" - he means he must be careful in case his feelings for Maud cause him to behave foolishly.

8

Perhaps the smile and tender tone
Came out of her pitying womanhood,
For am I not, am I not, here alone
So many a summer since she died,                         *255*
My mother, who was so gentle and good?
Living alone in an empty house,
Here half-hid in the gleaming wood,
Where I hear the dead at midday moan,
And the shrieking rush of the wainscot mouse,           *260*
And my own sad name in corners cried,
When the shiver of dancing leaves is thrown
About its echoing chambers wide,
Till a morbid hate and horror have grown
Of a world in which I have hardly mixt,                 *265*
And a morbid eating lichen fixt
On a heart half-turn'd to stone.

9

O heart of stone, are you flesh, and caught
By that you swore to withstand?
For what was it else within me wrought                   *270*
But, I fear, the new strong wine of love,
That made my tongue so stammer and trip
When I saw the treasured splendour, her hand,
Come sliding out of her sacred glove,
And the sunlight broke from her lip?                     *275*

10

I have play'd with her when a child;
She remembers it now we meet.
Ah well, well, well, I *may* be beguiled
By some coquettish deceit.
Yet, if she were not a cheat,                            *280*
If Maud were all that she seem'd,
And her smile had all that I dream'd,
Then the world were not so bitter
But a smile could make it sweet.

Synopsis

The narrator again alternates between distrust of, and love for, Maud. He thinks she may be kind to him out of pity for his loneliness since his parents died. The time he has spent in his empty house has hardened his heart, but Maud's arrival has caused his emotions to come back to life. Section six ends with the narrator hopeful that Maud might be genuine in her affections.

Stanzas 8 to 10

Stanza is another long verse, with sixteen lines, again showing a growing emotional intensity, as with the other long stanza, stanza six. The narrator still hopes that Maud is genuine, that her "smile and tender tone / Came out of her pitying womanhood", and were not false. In line three, the narrator's sadness is expressed in repetition, in "am I not, am I not, here alone", as the narrator remembers he has been living in isolation since his mother's death.

The rest of the stanza uses the imagery of Gothic fiction, as in the depictions of the narrator's father's terrible death in section one. The "empty house" which is "half-hid in the gleaming wood" is followed by a nightmarish vision. Tennyson concentrates upon the sounds of the empty house, and the fact that they appear to the narrator as sinister and haunted. The narrator says "I hear the dead at midday moan", with "moan" an example of onomatopoeia, the "m" sounds in both words making us imagine the eerie house's noises. Even the tiny animals are frightening, in the "shrieking rush of the wainscot mouse", which means a mouse living in the wooden panels. The narrator seems to hear his own name "in corners cried". A powerful use of the pathetic fallacy – when nature echoes the narrator's mood – comes in the description of the sounds of leaves in the wood, when "the shiver of dancing leaves is thrown / Around the echoing chambers wide". The "sh" sound of "shiver" echoes "shrieking" of the mouse. The word "shiver" is usually used when someone feels cold, rather than for the sound of leaves, and this clever use of words makes us feel the horror that the narrator feels when he is scared.

Stanza eight concludes with an image of a "lichen" or moss-like plant which has "fixt / On a heart half-turn'd to stone". This means that the narrator feels his emotions are being eaten up by solitude, and his heart closed to love.

Stanza nine takes this metaphor of a heart of stone, and shows the narrator's surprise that Maud has been able to break through his loneliness. He asks his heart "are you flesh", and then moves to another, more positive metaphor. He asks whether he was left tongue-tied or speechless in front of Maud's beauty by the "new strong wine of love". There are three stressed syllables in a row in "new strong wine" which shows the power of Maud's beauty. The narrator then concentrates upon Maud's hand, which he describes in very erotic terms, as a "treasured splendour" which he saw "sliding out of her sacred glove". The narrator often uses religious imagery in describing Maud, to express the power of her effect upon him. And, after the darkness of the imagery of the empty house, he ends this stanza with Maud standing for the power of the sun, telling us how "the sunlight broke from her lip".

The short, concluding stanza ten does not reject Maud, but comes to a more mature conclusion. The narrator remembers her as a child, and at his recent meeting with Maud, she recalled it too. The narrator still does not wholly trust her, but his expression of this is far less violent, and more reflective: "Ah well, well, well, I *may* be beguiled / By some coquettish deceit". The fact that the word "may" is in italics shows his doubt that she is guilty, and the rest of the passage concentrates further on the hope that she is genuine in her affections. A pretty rhyming couplet appears, which makes the verse suddenly more musical and hopeful: "If Maud were all that she seem'd / And her smile had all that I dream'd". The stanza ends with a repetition of the two lines that ended stanza five: "Then the world were not so bitter / But a smile could make it sweet".

The rhyme scheme here is very clever, and Tennyson uses it to show how Maud can bring harmony to the mental turmoil of the narrator. The word "bitter" rhymes with nothing in the stanza, but echoes the "t" sounds that end most of the lines, and has a harsh effect; Maud is the influence who can make everything "sweet". The word "sweet" rhymes with "deceit" and "cheat", but ending with "sweet" shows the triumph of love and kindness over the hard-hearted solitude that the narrator has endured.

1

DID I hear it half in a doze
  Long since, I know not where?
Did I dream it an hour ago,
  When asleep in this arm-chair?

2

Men were drinking together,
  Drinking and talking of me;    *290*
"Well, if it prove a girl, the boy
  Will have plenty: so let it be."

3

Is it an echo of something
  Read with a boy's delight,
Viziers nodding together    *295*
  In some Arabian night?

4

Strange, that I hear two men,
  Somewhere, talking of me;
"Well, if it prove a girl, my boy
  Will have plenty: so let it be."    *300*

Synopsis

In short section seven, the narrator remembers, as a small boy, overhearing a conversation between two men. One of them says that if the other's unborn child turns out to be a girl, she can marry his son. The narrator does not know if this was a dream or real. The implication is that one of the men is the narrator's father, and the other Maud's father; the section therefore implies that in some way Maud and the narrator are meant for each other.

Verse Form

The section is composed of four regular verses of four lines, rhyming ABCB; the lines are short, with between three and four stresses per line. The light, lilting quality of the verse gives it the nature of a nursery rhyme, which is in keeping with the fact it talks of a memory of childhood.

Stanzas 1 – 4

The first verse consists of a pair of questions that the narrator asks himself; he does not know whether he is remembering an incident, or simply remembering a dream. The phrase "half in a doze" means while on the point of going to sleep as a child (if Maud is just about to be born, he would be seven or eight). The language is deliberately simple and unpoetic, with such everyday words as "doze" and "armchair". The repetition of "Did I" in lines one and three shows the narrator's doubt about whether it is true or not.

The second stanza is more visual, and moves into describing the incident. The men are not identified, which adds to the mystery, but the reader soon can guess it is the narrator's father and Maud's father. The use of present participles in "drinking" and "talking" makes the scene appear vividly present to the reader, as if it is unfolding in front of them. Lines three and four are in reported speech, again making the incident lively and present: "If it prove a girl" means if the unborn child is female, she can marry the narrator. It is the narrator's father speaking here. This is before his financial ruin, so the "boy / Will have plenty" – namely he will be rich. The enjambment here between lines three and four adds to the illusion that this is a real conversation, rather than something poetic.

The third stanza introduces an image from literature about the Orient. As in section four, line 143, the narrator alludes to the famous work of Arab literature, the *One Thousand and One Nights*, also known as the *Arabian Nights*, which had come out in English in 1840. The narrator cannot be certain that he did not imagine this scene, basing it on "something / Read with a boy's delight". The narrator may have been recalling a tale about "Viziers nodding together / In some Arabian night". A vizier is an adviser to a powerful prince or sultan. The narrator might here be showing us that he is somehow romanticizing the story of him and Maud, to make it appear that they have always been meant for each other. We cannot be certain that this recollection is true, and it either shows the narrator's obsession with Maud that he fantasizes in this way, or that he and Maud genuinely had a connection that dates from before her birth. Either way, the narrator feels that they belong together.

The final stanza repeats much of stanza two, but subtly changes a couple of things. It omits the drinking, and starts with the word "Strange", as if the narrator does not truly understand the importance of what he is recalling – this is dramatic irony, when the reader or audience member knows more than the character, and is aware that what they are saying has a greater meaning, of which the character is unaware. Secondly, the last two lines are identical to stanza two, with only one change: "the boy / Will have plenty" becomes "my boy / Will have plenty". This perhaps shows that the narrator's memory is not completely reliable, and he is altering his memory to make sense of it, or perhaps simply that he is beginning to remember more clearly. Either way, this section adds mystery and depth to the story, and explains why the narrator has such powerful, and overwhelming feelings for Maud; it may be their love was fated before she was even born.

# VIII

SHE came to the village church,
And sat by a pillar alone;
An angel watching an urn
Wept over her, carved in stone;
And once, but once, she lifted her eyes,                    *305*
And suddenly, sweet, strangely blush'd
To find they were met by my own;
And suddenly, sweetly, my heart beat stronger
And thicker, until I heard no longer
The snowy-banded, dilettante,                               *310*
Delicate-handed priest intone;
And thought, is it pride, and mused and sigh'd
"No surely, now it cannot be pride."

Synopsis

Section eight is a very short section, and concentrates on a single incident. The narrator sees Maud alone in church, and catches her eye; she blushes, and the narrator is filled with emotion. He realizes that she might have feelings for him.

Verse Form

The whole section is a single stanza, of short lines, between seven and eleven syllables long. The lines lengthen whenever the narrator is talking about a strong emotional reaction. The rhyme scheme is quite loose, and Tennyson uses internal rhyme towards the end, again to signal emotion in the narrator.

Stanza 1

The stanza opens very visually; Maud has come to church alone, sitting by a pillar. This makes us think she is different to her family – a woman of her social standing would be more expected to come with her relatives – and perhaps has a secret. Her potential sadness is alluded to by a description of a statue next to her: "An angel watching an urn / Wept over her, carved in stone". The weeping angel is a funeral monument, and we are reminded of the theme of death in the poem.

Maud then looks at the narrator, and blushes. The repeated adverbs and "s" sounds in the line "suddenly, sweetly, strangely blush'd" show the narrator's heightened emotions; "sweet" echoes its use in section seven, when the narrator said a smile from Maud could make the whole world sweet for him. The narrator's reaction uses parallel language, with "suddenly, sweetly" his heart beating "stronger / And thicker" until he could "no longer" concentrates on the priest's sermon. The fact that the same words "suddenly" and "sweet" are repeated show in the narrator's mind he is now linked to Maud, and in sympathy with her.

Tennyson uses rhyme cleverly here. The fact that "stronger" and "longer" are both "feminine", or two-syllable rhymes, is very rare in the poem to date, and the two-beat rhythm of the rhyme echoes the narrator's stronger heartbeat, and accentuates his emotional reaction.

The narrator's description of the priest is very negative. He uses the metaphor "snowy-banded", which means that he either is wearing a white priest's collar, or has white hair; he calls him a "dilettante", which means an amateur or dabbler, who does not really understand what he is doing. Calling him "delicate-handed" means that he has never done any physical work, and implies his is weak. The narrator will criticize modern preachers further in part ten, and it is part of the theme of the poem that action, even violent action, is better than peace and inaction.

The last two lines are ambiguous. The internal rhyme shows the deep emotions of the narrator, sighing and musing (or thinking deeply) about either his or Maud's reaction: "And thought, is it pride, and mused and sigh'd / "No surely; now it cannot be pride." This could be read as: is it Maud's pride that causes her to blush at being seen looking at me? Or it could be read as: is it just my pride that causes my heart to beat stronger at Maud catching my eye? Either way, there is a new awakening to the potential that their relationship could have.

## IX

I WAS walking a mile,
More than a mile from the shore,    *315*
The sun look'd out with a smile
Betwixt the cloud and the moor,
And riding at set of day
Over the dark moor land,
Rapidly riding far away,    *320*
She waved to me with her hand.
There were two at her side,
Something flash'd in the sun,
Down by the hill I saw them ride,
In a moment they were gone:    *325*
Like a sudden spark
Struck vainly in the night,
Then returns the dark
With no more hope of light.

Synopsis

Section 9 is a short stanza, focusing on one incident. The narrator has been out walking at dusk, when he sees Maud riding on the moor; she waves at the narrator, but he notices that are two people accompanying her. The sight depresses him – as we will find out in section ten, the identity of her companions is vital for the plot.

Verse Form

This stanza is very regular, composed of sixteen lines, which can be broken into four sections, each rhyming ABAB. There are usually three stresses in each line, with fairly even short line lengths.

Stanza 1

The stanza opens with the narrator walking a mile from the shore. There is a very strong use of the pathetic fallacy here to describe the landscape, as nature mirrors the happy mood of the narrator. "The sun look'd out with a smile" imagines the sun itself happy, and is an example of personification. The narrator remains elated after catching Maud's eye in church in the previous section.

However, this happy state does not continue. The narrator catches sight of Maud "riding at set of day / Over the dark moor land". The introduction of the adjective "dark" here, after the happy sunlight, alerts us to a change in mood, to something less positive. The narrator repeats that Maud is "Rapidly riding far away", as if taking her further from him. The alliteration of "r" sounds makes the reader aware that the narrator is becoming more emotionally affected by what he is seeing.

At first view, all is well, as Maud signals to the narrator, waving at him, a friendly gesture. But there is a mystery: "There were two at her side". We learn who these two are in the next section, but now there is only a very mysterious image; "Something flash'd in the sun, / Down by the hill I saw them ride, / In a moment they were gone". We do not know what flashed in the sunlight, ore the identity of her companions, but the sight causes the narrator to become despairing. He uses a simile here, comparing the impact of what he has seen to a "spark" being "Struck vainly in the night", but which the night quickly swallows up "With no more hope of light". This means that what he has seen has ruined the potential happiness Maud represented, and the narrator is back in the darkness of his own isolation and depression.

Images of light are often associated with Maud in the poem, and also images of fire and warmth; section six (lines 204 – 210) used the very same image, of Maud kindling a "delicate spark" which might have grown into love, but which was extinguished by the narrator's mistrust. This short stanza cleverly reintroduces this image and shows that, in spite of everything, the narrator has not moved on, and is as unhappy as ever.

SICK, am I sick of a jealous dread?
Was not one of the two at her side
This new-made lord, whose splendour plucks
The slavish hat from the villager's head?
Whose old grandfather has lately died,
Gone to a blacker pit, for whom                    335
Grimy nakedness dragging his trucks
And laying his trams in a poison'd gloom
Wrought, till he crept from a gutted mine
Master of half a servile shire,
And left his coal all turn'd into gold             340
To a grandson, first of his noble line,
Rich in the grace all women desire,
Strong in the power that all men adore,
And simper and set their voices lower,
And soften as if to a girl, and hold               345
Awe-stricken breaths at a work divine,
Seeing his gewgaw castle shine,
New as his title, built last year,
There amid perky larches and pine,
And over the sullen-purple moor                    350
(Look at it) pricking a cockney ear.

Synopsis

In this first long stanza of section ten, the narrator realizes that one of the figures riding with Maud was a "new-made lord", a recently ennobled member of the aristocracy. The narrator tells us how the new-made lord's grandfather made his money from coal-mining, as did many newly rich people in the 19th century, helping drive the industrial revolution. The narrator snobbishly criticizes the vulgar castle the lord's family has built.

Verse Form

The whole section has stanzas of widely varying length, from two lines to twenty-two lines, showing the narrator veering between different emotions, from anger to depression; the lines are slightly longer than recent sections, usually eight or nine syllables, making them much less musical than sections in which Maud's love is central.

Stanza 1

The stanza opens with the narrator examining his own emotions: he is "sick of a jealous dread" as he realizes who one of the figures with Maud is. He is the "new-made lord" – a very wealthy mine-owner, with a new house in the area. The narrator is filled with scorn for this rival for Maud's affections. Many of the images that follow are obsessed with the origin of the wealth of the new-made lord, and betray the narrator's jealousy. He criticizes the way the lord's "splendour" causes a villager to raise his "slavish hat" to the lord. The word "slavish" means that the villager is acting as if he has no freedom, and is in thrall to the appearance and wealth of the lord.

The next few lines set out the background of the lord. The new-made lord's grandfather has just died, "gone to a blacker pit". This means gone to hell; it is also a pun because the family's wealth came from coal-mining. The increased demand for coal for factories during the Industrial Revolution in the early 19th century led to many families becoming rich very quickly. These people were called "new money" or the "nouveaux riches", which led to much resentment from poorer, but older-established noble and gentry families. Tennyson might have been expressing here some of the resentment he felt because his own family had been impoverished by his grandfather disinheriting his branch of the family, and making them fall down the social scale.

The narrator uses very specific details to illustrate the awful toll of coal-mining. He describes the workers underground, "Grimy nakedness dragging his trucks / And laying his trams in a poison'd gloom". The narrator here makes the place seem like hell itself, with "poison'd" echoing the use of the same word in section one, in connection with the corrupt business practices of Victorian England. The phrase "gutted mine" means that all the coal has been extracted, but "gutted" is usually used with animal carcasses, and is a horrid image. It is like the mine has damaged and killed the earth, leaving it an empty shell or a body with its insides taken out.

The narrator uses assonance to stress his distaste, as the grandfather "left his coal all turn'd into gold" to his grandson, the new-made lord. The narrator then launches into a long series of descriptions of the lord, and the effect that he has on the locals of the area. It first seems that the lord is very attractive, "Rich in the grace all women desire / Strong in the power that all men adore"; this is a very balanced and beautiful pair of lines. However the narrator then turns to criticize again the reaction of people to the lord. They "simper" or fawn upon the lord, lower their voices, "soften as if to a girl". He is implying that men become weak and effeminate in their toadying to the lord, with "Awe-stricken breaths at a word divine" being used ironically – the lord is not divine, just a man with the good luck to be born rich. We are back in the social criticism of part one of Maud, which focused upon the love of money of contemporary society.

The stanza ends with an image of the castle built by the new-made lord. It is "new as his title", which is again critical of his new money, and is described as "gewgaw", which means a showy and useless object, like an ornament. The landscape itself, in an example of the pathetic fallacy, responds to this sight in the same way as the narrator does. The moor is described as "sullen-purple", meaning it seems to sulk at the sight of the gaudy castle. The castle is personified as "pricking a cockney ear" or looking disdainfully at its surroundings, acting as if it superior. A cockney is usually used to describe a native Londoner, but here it means low-born, rude and out of place. (Cockneys in the 19th century also had a reputation for pride and cheek). The narrator uses this to image to show how everything related to the new-made lord is unpleasant, arrogant and artificial, but it mostly betrays the narrator's own jealousy.

What, has he found my jewel out?
For one of the two that rode at her side
Bound for the Hall, I am sure was he:
Bound for the Hall, and I think for a bride.          *355*
Blithe would her brother's acceptance be.
Maud could be gracious too, no doubt,
To a lord, a captain, a padded shape,
A bought commission, a waxen face,
A rabbit mouth that is ever agape—                    *360*
Bought? what is it he cannot buy?
And therefore splenetic, personal, base,
A wounded thing with a rancorous cry,
At war with myself and a wretched race,
Sick, sick to the heart of life, am I.                *365*

Synopsis

The narrator realizes that the new-made lord, riding with Maud and her brother, has probably been promised her hand in marriage. The stanza shows his anger and dejection at this thought.

Stanza 2

The stanza opens with the narrator describing Maud as "my jewel"; this image both expresses how precious he thinks Maud is, but also that she is "my" jewel – the narrator regards her as belonging to him. He does not allow the possibility Maud might have feelings for the lord.

The narrator is certain now that the man riding alongside Maud was the lord. He repeats the phrase "Bound for the Hall" in lines three and four, signaling his obsession with the lord, now that Maud is, her fears, promised to him as a bride. The word "Bound" has two meanings here. It means to be on the way somewhere, as in "homeward bound", but is also mean tied into an agreement. It is also used in an old-fashioned phrase for a wedding, "bound together in holy matrimony". He is therefore obsessed by the possibility of Maud being married to someone else.

The middle of the stanza is obsessed with jealousy, and is made up of a number of descriptions of the lord, which show the narrator's hatred. He says that Maud could be "gracious" to "a lord, a captain", which seem like normal descriptions, but then the narrator starts to rant and criticize. The lord is a "padded shape", meaning that he has a poor physique which is disguised by clothes. He has a "bought commission", which means that his rank as a soldier has not been earned by valour, but purchased with this family's money, which was possible in the 19ᵗʰ century. The narrator then gets even more personal in his attack, with a description of "a waxen face / A rabbit mouth that is ever agape". This means the lord has an expression like a rabbit, mouth open, appearing ugly.

The narrator follows up this personal attack with an attack on the new-made lord's wealth: "Bought? what is it he cannot buy?" This implies that Maud has been bought by his money, making her like a prostitute. This fear causes the narrator to wallow in self-pity for the last four lines of the stanza. He describes himself as "splenetic", which is a word meaning angry, as well as "base", or inferior. His next image has more pathos, making the reader feel sorry for himself: he is "A wounded thing with a rancorous cry", like a wounded animal crying out horribly in its pain. The narrator then returns to the wider social criticism of previous stanzas, using war imagery to describe how out of step he feels with the age and the people with whom he lives: "At war with myself and a wretched race", the "r" sounds repeated at the end using alliteration to show how upset he is.

The final line repeats the words "Sick, sick" from the opening of stanza one of this section, but it is not just a "jealous dread" he has; the narrator is "sick to the heart of life".

Last week came one to the county town,
To preach our poor little army down,
And play the game of the despot kings,
Tho' the state has done it and thrice as well:
This broad-brimm'd hawker of holy things,     *370*
Whose ear is stuff'd with his cotton, and rings
Even in dreams to the chink of his pence,
This huckster put down war! can he tell
Whether war be a cause or a consequence?
Put down the passions that make earth Hell!     *375*
Down with ambition, avarice, pride,
Jealousy, down! cut off from the mind
The bitter springs of anger and fear;
Down too, down at your own fireside,
With the evil tongue, and the evil ear,     *380*
For each is at war with mankind.

Synopsis

The narrator suddenly breaks away from talking about Maud to return to the social commentary of part one, in which he had praised war and criticized peace. He recalls that a preacher came to town last week, preaching against war. The narrator criticizes the preacher for concentrating upon business and commerce. The stanza ends with a confused list of the emotions that the narrator feels are wrong with the modern age.

Stanza 3

The narrator recalls that a travelling preacher came to their local "county town / To preach our poor little army down". This means to criticize the British Army. The narrator calls such criticism "the game of the despot kings", which means that he feels that this so-called Christian, to him, is as bad as a tyrant for holding such views. The narrator then broadens his criticism to the then current British government, who have also held the army in low regard, but perhaps even more damagingly than the church: "the state has done it and thrice as well".

The preacher is described in such a way as to make it clear he is not a member of the official Church of England, but a non-conformist with pacifist views. This means a type of Christianity which is more independent and anti-war, such as the Society of Friends, commonly known as the "Quakers", or the Methodists, who had broken away from the Church of England. The preacher is a "broad-brimm'd hawker of holy things", which firstly means he wears a large hat, such as were worn by non-conformists such as Quakers. The narrator fixates on money here as a "hawker" means someone who travels and sells door-to-door. This recalls the criticism of business in part one of *Maud*.

The narrator continues to describe the preacher in terms of someone who is obsessed by money: his "ear is stuff'd with cotton". This alludes to the very rich cotton mill owners of the North of England, many of whom were non-conformist, pacifist Christians. Indeed many famous British businesses, such as Cadbury's and Quaker Oats, were founded in the 19th century in this way. The narrator though continues viciously to state that the preacher's ear's ring "to the chink of his pence", meaning he dreams of money. He finally tells us that "This huckster puts down war!" A huckster means a confidence trickster or scammer.

The narrator then gives a very interesting viewpoint: "can he tell / Whether war be a cause or a consequence?" This means does war create misery, or does human misery create war? This is a very depressing position, and we can see how low the narrator's spirits are.

The rest of the stanza builds to a climax of unhappiness. The narrator lists a series of very negative emotions, with the strong imperative or command "down" repeated, as if he is trying to ward them off: "ambition, avarice, pride / Jealousy, down!" He uses the violent word "cut off" to describe how he would like to rid himself from "The bitter springs of anger and fear". The narrator then seems to confront the reader directly, which is a very powerful technique to make us understand his dark emotions: "Down too, down at your own fireside, / With the evil tongue, and the evil ear". This means that he wants to make us understand how our own words and thoughts contribute to the evil of the world. The final line has an image of universal conflict: "For each is at war with mankind". This means that everyone is angry with everyone else.

4

I wish I could hear again
The chivalrous battle-song
That she warbled alone in her joy!
I might persuade myself then                    *385*
She would not do herself this great wrong,
To take a wanton dissolute boy
For a man and leader of men.

5

Ah God, for a man with heart, head, hand,
Like some of the simple great ones gone        *390*
For ever and ever by,
One still strong man in a blatant land,
Whatever they call him, what care I,
Aristocrat, democrat, plutocrat—one
Who can rule and dare not lie.                  *395*

6

And ah for a man to rise in me,
That the man I am may cease to be!

Synopsis

The narrator wishes he could hear Maud singing the song from section five, in which she glorified war, as this would reassure him that Maud did not wish to marry the weak new-made lord. The narrator then wishes for a strong leader to come and transform Britain; he finishes by an anguished plea that he himself might change and become a better man.

Stanzas 4 – 6

Stanza four is much shorter in length than the preceding ones, at only six lines. It also has much shorter lines, making it more lyrical. This matches the subject matter, as the narrator is recalling Maud's song of section five; this section had shorter lines also, here only seven syllables. The narrator wishes he could hear the song again. He describes it as "The chivalrous battle-song / That she warbled alone in her joy". The word chivalrous refers to chivalry, a code of behaviour from the middle ages which encouraged honour and bravery amongst the nobility. Its most famous example is found in the stories of King Arthur and the Knights of the Round Table, which had become very popular again in the 19th century, often as a contrast to the growing ugliness of modern urban life. Tennyson himself re-wrote many Arthurian tales in his *Idylls of the King*, a series of poems he worked on much of his life. In these tales, knights are inspired to feats in battle through love for unattainable, beautiful women; however, at the heart of the stories is the illicit love between the greatest knight, Lancelot, and Arthur's queen, Guinevere; this reminds us that love is destructive, as well as an ennobling force.

The narrator wishes he could hear Maud's song again to persuade him that she will not take the new-made lord to be her husband. This is because in the narrator's view he is a "wanton dissolute boy", which means badly behaved and unable to control himself. The lord cannot be a "man and leader of men".

The next stanza is disturbing for readers who approach the poem after the events of the 20th century, because Tennyson seems to be calling for dictator to take control of the country. He starts by asking for God for a man with "heart, head, hand", like one of the "simple great ones gone"; this means a ruler with both intelligence and strength, "one still strong man in a blatant land". The word blatant means where things are done without shame or even attempt to cover up wrong-doing. But then the narrator finishes with "Aristocrat, democrat, plutocrat – one / Who can rule and dare not lie". The enjambment here shows the narrator is very emotional. He does not care if democracy, or the rule of the people, is not upheld. He would accept an aristocrat – or a member of the nobility – or a plutocrat, which means government by a wealthy elite. In 19th century Britain, many people were denied the vote, including all women and many poorer men, and there had been riots in 1819 in Manchester in demands for change and more democracy. Britain had also been involved for many years in fighting the Emperor Napoleon in France, as he had tried to take over Europe. Napoleon was ultimately defeated in 1815 at Waterloo, but the memory of his ambition remained in Britain. In 1848, more recently for Tennyson, there had been revolutions across Europe as people wanted more power for themselves. Also, reading this stanza from a modern viewpoint, after seeing the tyranny of such dictators as Hitler, Stalin and Mao in countries without democracy, we might not be as sympathetic to this possibility as the narrator is.

The last stanza, however, shows what the narrator is really agitated by; he is perhaps not talking about government at all, but about himself. He feels that he needs renewal; when he has been talking about the corruption of the country, perhaps he really means that he himself feels corrupt. His talk of politics is a metaphor for himself, and the strong man he wishes to rise up, is in fact his better self. This is a very short stanza, only two lines in a rhyming couplet, to bring this anguished section of the poem to a conclusion: "And ah for a man to rise in me, / That the man I am may cease to be!" The use of the exclamation "ah" here cleverly shows the narrator's emotions, as if the narrator were really speaking, or was unable to contain himself.

## XI

### 1

O LET the solid ground
  Not fail beneath my feet
Before my life has found     *400*
  What some have found so sweet;
Then let come what come may,
What matter if I go mad,
I shall have had my day.

### 2     *405*

Let the sweet heavens endure,
  Not close and darken above me
Before I am quite sure
  That there is one to love me;
Then let come what come may
To a life that has been so sad,     *410*
I shall have had my day.

Synopsis

The narrator prays that he will find love before he goes mad. If he finds love after such a sad life, he does not care what happens to him.

Verse Form

Section eleven consists of two short stanzas, with a high level of repetition between them. The short lines have three stresses each, and rhyme ABAB CDC. The gentle, lyrical nature of this stanza form contrasts with the very sad, resigned tone, creating a very strong sense of pathos.

Stanzas 1-2

The poem opens as if it were a prayer, though God is not mentioned. The word "O" vividly makes it seem like the narrator is talking aloud. The verb "let" is in the imperative, the narrator asking for something. The first two lines run on with a very clear example of enjambment: "O let the solid ground / Not fail beneath my feet". The enjambment is unexpected, the word "Not" falling oddly at the beginning of the line, and it gives a sense of unease to this line. The normal word order for this sentence might be "let not the solid ground fail beneath my feet". It is as if the narrator were so frightened about the earth melting under him as he descends into madness, that the sentence structure itself becomes unstable and unexpected. This form of changing normal sentence structure for poetic effect is sometimes also called inversion.

The narrator is praying that, before this descent into madness, he will have "found / What some have found so sweet". The use of the word "sweet" here alerts us to the fact he is talking about Maud's love, echoing section six, lines 283-284: ("Then the world were not so bitter / But a smile could make it sweet.").

The first four lines of the first stanza form a regular rhyming quatrain. The final three lines form another separate unit, but here one word does not rhyme with other line endings in the stanza, the word "mad" in the penultimate line. This makes it stand out very strongly, as madness is the greatest fear now striking the narrator. The narrator, however, does not seem to care, as long as he finds love with Maud: "let come what come may", he says, and in the final line he appears completely resigned, using a very rare tense, the future perfect: "I shall have had my day". This odd tense mixes future and past together, and we see that the narrator is imagining a time when he will no long exist. The stanza therefore seems to point to death as well as madness, in spite of its gentle sounds and regular rhymes. There is an old English proverb alluded to here as well: "every dog has its day", meaning that even unlucky people will enjoy at least one moment of triumph.

Stanza two opens with another imperative, and another statement which sounds like a prayer: "Let the sweet heavens endure". This initially appears very positive. However, the narrator quickly changes to a blacker mood: "Not close and darken above me". The word "Not" reappears at the start of line two, as in the first stanza, which signals that the message will be the same: the narrator is careless of his own future if he can finally find love. He prays that the clouds do not darken his life "Before I am quite sure / That there is one to love me". The rhyme here is a feminine rhyme – one with two syllables, "above me" and "love me". This is the only feminine rhyme in the section (and they are very rare in *Maud* as a whole) so it seems to signal that it is a feminine presence – Maud – who is hinted at here.

The final three lines are almost identical to the first stanza, and only the penultimate lines change, "mad" in the first stanza changing to "sad" in the second. The whole line in the second stanza is "To a life that has been so sad", which shows that the narrator feels his whole life to this point has been filled with misery. The mad/sad rhyme is so delayed, between the first and second stanza, that it makes us appreciate how delayed has been the arrival of happiness in the narrator's life, and that he is hoping that his despair can finally, after so long, be lifted through his love of Maud.

# XII

## 1

BIRDS in the high Hall-garden
   When twilight was falling,
Maud, Maud, Maud, Maud,
   They were crying and calling.    *415*

## 2

Where was Maud? in our wood;
   And I, who else, was with her,
Gathering woodland lilies,
   Myriads blow together.

## 3        *420*

Birds in our wood sang
   Ringing thro' the valleys,
Maud is here, here, here
   In among the lilies.

## 4

I kiss'd her slender hand,
   She took the kiss sedately;    *425*
Maud is not seventeen,
   But she is tall and stately.

Synopsis

The narrator describes, in light, lyrical verse, how birds in the wood seem to call Maud's name. The narrator also dwells upon Maud's beauty and her youth.

Verse Form

Section twelve is composed of eight regular stanzas, rhyming ABCB throughout. The lines are very short – at four syllables in places, the shortest in the poem to date – and all have a feminine rhyme, composed of more than one syllable (for example, "falling" and "calling"). This makes the poem extremely musical and unlike normal speech, which expresses the narrator's high spirits and love.

Stanzas 1-4

The first stanza plunges the reader directly into a description of the natural world, setting the scene as in the garden of Maud's home (the "high Hall-garden"), at twilight. The third stanza uses onomatopoeia, as it mimics the sound of birdsong, repeating Maud's name four times: "Maud, Maud, Maud, Maud". This also signals how obsessed the narrator is by Maud, in that everything reminds him of her. The birds are also "crying and calling", the word "crying" having a double meaning, of tears and weeping, reminding the reader that joy and tragedy in *Maud* are mixed together.

The second verse opens with a rhetorical question, which the narrator answers with a sense of pride: "Where was Maud? in our wood; / And I, who else, was with her". The fact the narrator uses the word "our wood" shows pride, but the phrase "who else" shows his insecurity: we know that Maud has in fact another suitor, the new-made lord. The narrator carries on to describe what Maud is doing. She is gathering lilies, as "myriads" or a large number can be found in the wood. The use of flower imagery here, and in the third stanza, is important. Lilies, associated with the Virgin Mary, symbolize purity, but also have connotations of death, being a common flower for funerals. This gives a sinister undertone to the verse, and hints at future tragedy.

The third verse takes the imagery of flowers and bird, and weaves them together; this is another example of the pathetic fallacy, where nature echoes the emotions of the narrator. The birdsong and the flowers are all expressive of his love for Maud. Again there is onomatopoeia, as the birds' refrain of "Maud is here, here, here / In among the lilies" again sounds like birdcall. The rhyme here, of "lilies" and "valleys" is not a perfect feminine rhyme, as the first vowel sound is wrong; this imperfect rhyme, a slight note of discord, prepares us for the content of stanzas seven and eight, in which the narrator's happiness is threatened by the arrival of the new-made lord to woo Maud.

The fourth stanza introduces us to some descriptions of Maud. The language here is very archaic, and the narrator is echoing English love poetry of the past, particularly of the medieval age of chivalry, or lyrical poetry of the 16th century. As noted above, Tennyson, in common with other Victorian artists and writers, uses echoes of medieval and renaissance poetry to contrast with the ugliness of their age. Here we have the narrator telling us that "I kiss'd her slender hand / She took the kiss sedately", which means that the relationship seems to remain at a chaste respectful level. Maud is "not seventeen / But she is tall and stately". This means that Maud is only sixteen years old, the narrator twenty-five. Sixteen, in Victorian times, was not seen as too young to marry. The age of sexual consent was only fixed at sixteen in 1885, and before that earlier marriage was not unusual.

The narrator is therefore keen to reassure the reader that Maud is not child-like, but a fully-grown woman, being "tall and stately". But we are reminded how young and inexperienced she is, and we are aware that she is caught between her family's wish to marry her off for money, and the love of the narrator, who is an intense and troubled young man, with no money. This love triangle, and its underlying clash between heart and duty, is very typical of the situation many women found themselves in during the 19th century.

I to cry out on pride
   Who have won her favour!
O Maud were sure of Heaven      *430*
   If lowliness could save her.

6

I know the way she went
   Home with her maiden posy,
For her feet have touch'd the meadows
   And left the daisies rosy.      *435*

7

Birds in the high Hall-garden
   Were crying and calling to her,
Where is Maud, Maud, Maud?
   One is come to woo her.

8      *440*

Look, a horse at the door,
   And little King Charley snarling,
Go back, my lord, across the moor,
   You are not her darling.

Synopsis

The narrator continues with his praise of Maud's beauty, but the final stanza introduces the dark shadow of Maud's courtship by the new-made lord, the narrator's rich rival.

Stanzas 5-8

Stanza five continues with the courtly, old-fashioned poetic language of stanza four. The narrator wishes to cry out in pride because he has "won her favour". This is taken from the language of medieval chivalry, where a noble lady would give her "favour" to a knight about to enter combat. In this context favour means a piece of jewelry, or clothing, to show her love to the knight, and express her desire for him to return from battle or jousting. This therefore has an ominous subtext: that the narrator might have to be involved in a fight for Maud's love. Indeed the narrator does have a rival – the new-made lord. The rest of the stanza ends with a realization of the narrator's humble origin: "O Maud were sure of Heaven / If lowliness could save here", meaning that Maud's honour would be assured if she would lower herself to marry the poverty-stricken narrator.

Again, stanza six continues to use a very artificial and affected vocabulary, which shows that the narrator is so intoxicated with love for Maud that he is losing his grasp on reality. Maud has gone home "with her maiden posy", which implies that she is still a virgin and therefore he has not had sex with her, and his love remains pure. However this is followed with a very unreal and almost ridiculous image: "her feet have touch'd the meadows / And left the daisies rosy". This unreal, fairy-tale vocabulary is a very abrupt shift in tone from the violent social criticism of earlier sections, or the harrowing, melancholy passages where the narrator fears he is going mad. The fact that the narrator veers from one extreme to the other in the poem alerts us to his mental instability.

The next stanza, while echoing stanza one, brings once more a disruptive element into the narrator's fairy-tale verses. Again, there is a use of onomatopoeia as we hear of birds in the Hall Garden, calling her name, but here there are looking for her because she has a suitor: "Where is Maud, Maud, Maud / One is come to woo her".

In stanza eight, we learn that this suitor is not the narrator, but the new-made lord himself. The poem uses an imperative form of the verb to startle the reader and force us into taking notice of the scene: "Look, a horse at the door / And little King Charley snarling". This means that Maud's King Charles spaniel is growling at the lord – a comic touch, but which makes us think that even her dog recognizes that Maud should not marry him, and the lord is untrustworthy. The last two lines are bitter, and express the narrator's possessiveness: Maud is his, not the lord's: "Go back, my lord, across the moor / You are not her darling". The implication is that the narrator is Maud's darling.

## XIII

### 1

SCORN'D, to be scorn'd by one that I scorn,
Is that a matter to make me fret? *445*
That a calamity hard to be borne?
Well, he may live to hate me yet.
Fool that I am to be vext with his pride!
I past him, I was crossing his lands;
He stood on the path a little aside; *450*
His face, as I grant, in spite of spite
Has a broad-blown comeliness, red and white,
And six feet two, as I think, he stands;
But his essences turn'd the live air sick,
And barbarous opulence jewel-thick *455*
Sunn'd itself on his breast and his hands.

### 2

Who shall call me ungentle, unfair,
I long'd so heartily then and there
To give him the grasp of fellowship;
But while I past he was humming an air, *460*
Stopt, and then with a riding whip
Leisurely tapping a glossy boot,
And curving a contumelious lip,
Gorgonised me from head to foot
With a stony British stare. *465*

50

Synopsis

The narrator recalls meeting Maud's brother while out walking; the narrator describes the brother's appearance in negative terms. The brother looks on the narrator with scorn.

Verse Form

Section thirteen returns to longer lines of seven to nine syllables after the short, lyrical verses of section twelve. There are four stanzas of widely different lengths, between two and twenty-one lines. This more irregular and prosaic form of verse suits the grim subject matter, which is the narrator's anger at Maud's brother, which expresses itself in violent and bizarre images.

Stanzas 1 and 2

Stanza one opens with a rhetorical question: why should the narrator be upset that Maud's brother despises or scorns him, given that the narrator hates him in return? However, it is quickly clear that the narrator is very upset indeed. He repeats the word "scorn'd" twice, and the word "scorn" once, in the first line alone: "Scorn'd, to be scorn'd by one that I scorn, / Is that a matter to make me fret?" The harsh sibilance of the "sc" sounds is very unpleasant to the ear, and emphasizes how upset the narrator is. Ominously, he seems to threaten the brother: "he may live to hate me yet".

The reason the narrator is so angry becomes obvious in the rest of this stanza, especially in the second stanza. The narrator describes meeting Maud's brother, as the narrator was walking over Maud's family lands. The narrator, although he is angry, recognizes the brother is handsome, but with coarse features and a ruddy complexion, a "broad-blown comeliness, red and white". The brother is tall as well as handsome – six foot two – but the narrator cannot resist describing him in extremely unflattering imagery. The narrator says that the brother's perfume is overpowering: "his essences turn'd the live air sick", and the brother's clothes are extravagant and unpleasantly gaudy: "barbarous opulence jewel-thick / Sunn'd itself on his breast and his hands". The word barbarous means uncivilized, and the narrator is implying there is something foreign and un-English in the way he is dressing. The narrator's efforts to convince us of the handsome brother's ugliness perhaps really shows the narrator's jealousy.

Stanza two gives even more reasons for the narrator's anger: Maud's brother has rejected his friendly advances. The narrator was not "ungentle" or "unfair", but wished to make peace and embrace the brother: "I long'd so heartily then and there / To give him the grasp of fellowship". But the brother's behaviour is extremely arrogant. While the narrator is passing by, the brother ignores him, "humming an air" arrogantly, and tapping his boot with a riding crop or whip.

However, this is not the worst of the brother's behaviour: he gives the narrator a terrible stare. The language here is very interesting. The brother curves a "contumelious lip". This is a very rare adjective which means scornful or insulting. It is very difficult to say this word without curling your lip, and the fact that it is polysyllabic, or a very long word, adds to its effect. The brother then gives a very fierce look to the narrator, which fixes him to the spot: "Gorgonised me from head to foot / With a stony British stare". The word "gorgonised" is another unusual word which means to turn to stone. It is taken from ancient Greek mythology. A gorgon was a woman with wings, and hair made of snakes, whose gaze could turn a man to stone. The most famous gorgon, Medusa, was defeated by the hero Perseus, who used his shield as a mirror so that he could avoid looking directly at her eyes as he approached; he cut off Medusa's head, and subsequently used it as a weapon. The use of such a powerful allusion signifies how strongly the narrator was affected by the brother's spite, but there is also a hint of grim humour in the use of the phrase "stony British stare", as we are not in the world of Greek gods, but of the English countryside. This is perhaps a use of the literary technique of bathos, where an everyday and petty event (a harsh look) is described in mock-heroic terms, which serves to deflate pomposity and make things seem funny.

Why sits he here in his father's chair?
That old man never comes to his place:
Shall I believe him ashamed to be seen?
For only once, in the village street,
Last year, I caught a glimpse of his face,        *470*
A gray old wolf and a lean.
Scarcely, now, would I call him a cheat:
For then, perhaps, as a child of deceit,
She might by a true descent be untrue;
And Maud is as true as Maud is sweet:        *475*
Tho' I fancy her sweetness only due
To the sweeter blood by the other side;
Her mother has been a thing complete,
However she came to be so allied.
And fair without, faithful within,        *480*
Maud to him is nothing akin:
Some peculiar mystic grace
Made her only the child of her mother,
And heap'd the whole inherited sin
On that huge scapegoat of the race,        *485*
All, all upon the brother.

Peace, angry spirit, and let him be!
Has not his sister smiled on me?

Synopsis

The narrator wonders why the brother now appears to be head of Maud's family, while her father is nowhere to be seen. The narrator fears that Maud will inherit her father's deceitful nature. However, the narrator then speculates that Maud is in some way the child of her mother only, and will escape the family's evil nature, which becomes concentrated in the brother.

Stanzas 3 and 4

Stanza three is very long, at twenty one lines; it is long because it shows the narrator struggling at length with reconciling his love for the pure, sweet Maud, with his hatred for her father and brother. It opens with two questions – firstly, why is the brother here at the Manor, rather than his father, and secondly, is the absence due to a sense of shame? The narrator does not answer either question, and uses a metaphor drawn from nature to describe the father, whom he saw in the village street last year. He is "a gray old wolf and a lean". This image makes the old man appear both dangerous – a wolf is a predator – but also old and perhaps vulnerable due to age. This contrasts strongly with the portrayal of the son as large, imposing and handsome.

The narrator struggles with calling Maud's father a cheat, because this reflects badly upon Maud: "perhaps, as a child of deceit, / She might by a true descent be untrue". This means that as her father's legitimate daughter, she inherits his bad characteristics. Science in the 19th century was obsessed by "heredity", which meant that children not only inherited physical characteristics, but moral characteristics from their parents. Nowadays, scientists are aware that the situation is more complex and that how a child is brought up is much more important, and the idea that people cannot escape the sins and crimes of the family is no longer accepted.

The narrator is in a dilemma, though, as he seems to believe that it is not possible to escape one's heredity – which, ironically, might mark him out as doomed, given his father's madness and suicide. He has to find an imaginative way out, which is to imagine that Maud is actually genuinely sweet and good because she inherits her mother's disposition only. The adjective "sweet" is repeated a number of times, picking up its use as a constant way of discussing Maud in previous sections. Here we are told that "Maud is as true as Maud is sweet", because "her sweetness [is] only due / To the sweeter blood on the other side", namely her mother. Maud is "fair without, and faithful within", a true echo of her perfect mother, who was "complete", not lacking in any grace.

The narrator cannot leave it at that. He is repulsed by the idea that Maud is in any way related to her father, so he uses an image which seems a strange echo of Christianity's Virgin Birth, when Jesus Christ was born of Mary without an earthly father. The narrator says that "Some peculiar mystic grace / Made her only the child of her mother". This strange image implies that Maud is now magically free of the father's sin. This almost blasphemous thought for the time emphasizes the narrator's desperation to prove Maud is good and honest. This obsession surfaces again as the narrator then turns towards the brother. If Maud is wholly the child of her mother, why is the brother not also at least partly good, in the same way? Here, the narrator decides that the brother is the inheritor of all the family's bad characteristics. His birth "heap'd the whole inherited sin / On that huge scapegoat of the race / All, all upon the brother". The repetition of "All, all" signals the narrator's emotional distress here.

The word "scapegoat" means someone who takes the blame for others, often unfairly. The reference is Biblical, to the Old Testament book of Leviticus. On Yom Kippur, or the Jewish Day of Atonement, a goat is released into the wilderness after the Jewish High Priest symbolically lays all of the sins of the congregation on it. The narrator's use of this Biblical reference, after the strange imagining of Maud's birth, shows the extent of his desire to prove that Maud is good. However, the use of scapegoat makes us think that the narrator is being unfair in laying all faults at the feet of Maud's brother; the scapegoat is an innocent animal, caught up in a wider religious ceremony.

The final stanza of this section is very short, only two lines, in which the narrator seems to come to his senses and realizes that he has over-reacted: "Peace, angry spirit, and let him be! / Has not his sister smiled at me?" The rhyming couplet brings that very emotional section to a calmer conclusion, with the hope that Maud's love can smooth away all troubles.

# XIV

## 1

MAUD has a garden of roses
And lilies fair on a lawn;                                      *490*
There she walks in her state
And tends upon bed and bower,
And thither I climb'd at dawn
And stood by her garden-gate;
A lion ramps at the top,                                        *495*
He is claspt by a passion-flower.

## 2

Maud's own little oak-room
(Which Maud, like a precious stone
Set in the heart of the carven gloom,
Lights with herself, when alone                                *500*
She sits by her music and books,
And her brother lingers late
With a roystering company) looks
Upon Maud's own garden gate:
And I thought as I stood, if a hand, as white                   *505*
As ocean-foam in the moon, were laid
On the hasp of the window, and my Delight
Had a sudden desire, like a glorious ghost, to glide,
Like a beam of the seventh Heaven, down to my side,
There were but a step to be made.                              *510*

Synopsis

The narrator sneaks to Maud's house at dawn and observes her in her room from the garden gate. He imagines Maud's hand on the window-sill as he looks, and is transported with delight.

Verse Form

Section fourteen is very irregular, composed of two short stanzas and two long stanzas, with lines ranging from six to fourteen lines, the line-length extending whenever the narrator is overtaken by powerful emotions.

Stanza 1-2

Stanza one starts with a simple, lyrical line, using flower imagery: "Maud has a garden of roses / And lilies fair on a lawn". The flowers have different symbolic meanings in the poem *Maud* as a whole; the rose symbolizing passion, desire and blood, the lily virginity, beauty, as well as death. These are the key preoccupations of the whole poem – do love and desire bring life and happiness, or is passion dangerous and leads to madness and death? The poem is ambivalent at this stage, and the reader is unsure what the outcome will be.

Stanza one continues with a description of Maud walking in the garden. The narrator is, in effect, spying on her, presumably without her knowledge; this might make us think that his love for her is one-sided, and that he is only infatuated. Indeed he seems to be under her power. This is shown in a clever image that finishes the stanza. The narrator describes a statue by the gate, where "A lion ramps at the top, / He is claspt by a passion-flower". The word "ramps" means a lion rampant, or on his back legs. A lion rampant was often used on coats of arms in the medieval period, and is another example in *Maud* of the imagery of courtly love being used. But this lion is not powerful, he is overpowered by a simple flower; this symbolizes that the strong are brought down by beauty. It is similar to an image in section six, where Maud was described as having "her lion roll in a silken net". Also, the word passion in passion-flower has a second meaning of death, as in the passion of Jesus Christ, where He was killed on the cross. The passion-flower is so named because when it was discovered in America, the Catholic priests who found it believed that the markings on the flower resembled parts of the Biblical story – such as five stamens symbolizing the five wounds of Christ. By showing the lion overwhelmed by such symbols of suffering, Tennyson is showing here how love can lead and ultimately to death.

Stanza two continues with the narrator spying on Maud, like a voyeur, or someone who is sexually excited by observing someone when hidden. He fixates upon Maud's bedroom. The narrator re-introduces the image of Maud as a precious jewel, to contrast again with her brother. She is a "precious stone" amid the "carven gloom", or dark wood of her house. In an odd image, she "Lights with herself" the dark chamber, implying she has a magical quality that can banish darkness. This shows the narrator idealizing her again. The brother, on the other hand, "lingers late / With a roystering company", partying late into the night with unsuitable friends.

The narrator then has a mystical vision of Maud, and to signal a change in focus the verse form here becomes very different. There is firstly a use of enjambment to highlights this shift into a greater level of emotion, as he describes Maud using a simile of "a hand, as white / As ocean-foam in the moon". The simile being split across two lines gives it a strong emphasis. He is contrasting the whiteness of Maud to her brother's red face and the darkness of the house, ocean-foam and the moon being two of the palest things possible. This shows how beautiful and different Maud is. Then the verse length becomes longer, increasing from six syllables up to fourteen. This shows the poet carried away by his vision of Maud. This vision is a fantasy, in which he imagines that Maud, his "Delight", could if she wished float like a ghost or moonbeam down to him, through the air to where he is waiting by the garden gate. The use of "g" alliteration in the phrase "like a glorious ghost, to glide / Like a beam of the seventh Heaven, down to my side" draws further attention to the startling image, and the skillful use of enjambment in this the simile of Maud being like a moonbeam shows the narrator's heightened emotions, and his aroused imagination.

We use the phrase today "to be in seventh Heaven" to describe being ecstatically happy, which is what the narrator is also doing. The concept of seven levels of Heaven, with the seventh the highest, is an ancient one in the Abrahamic faiths of Judaism, Christianity, and Islam, and is mentioned in the Old Testament book of Enoch. However, to imagine one's loved one as a ghost is morbid, and shows again that love and death and mixed up in the poet's mind; this also points forward to the narrator's haunting in part two.

3

The fancy flatter'd my mind,
And again seem'd overbold;
Now I thought that she cared for me,
Now I thought she was kind
Only because she was cold.

4

I heard no sound where I stood
But the rivulet on from the lawn
Running down to my own dark wood;
Or the voice of the long sea-wave as it swell'd
Now and then in the dim-gray dawn;
But I look'd, and round, all round the house I beheld
The death-white curtain drawn;
Felt a horror over me creep,
Prickle my skin and catch my breath,
Knew that the death-white curtain meant but sleep,
Yet I shudder'd and thought like a fool of the sleep of death.

*515*

*520*

*525*

56

Synopsis

The narrator is again uncertain whether Maud genuinely loves him or is just being cold, submitting to his love. The sight of Maud's house in the the moonlight horrifies the narrator, who does not think of the people living in the house being asleep, but thinks only of death.

Stanzas 3 – 4

Stanza three is a very short stanza, after the lengthy second stanza, with its extravagant imagery. The narrator dismisses the "fancy" he had of Maud stepping down to him on a moonbeam, calling it "overbold", or presumptuous. Instead, the narrator is plunged into a depression. He starts using the past tense in talking about Maud's feelings for him. He "thought that she cared" and "thought she was kind", as if their love is already over. He now thinks he was mistaken in his view of Maud, feeling perhaps he misinterpreted her "because she was cold". The line "I thought that she cared for me" has no rhyme, making it stand out; this echoes how lonely the narrator suddenly appears, without a genuine companion. This is a very clever technique that Tennyson uses to emphasize the narrator's isolation.

After this simple stanza, which has no imagery, the next stanza is again long, and filled with metaphors. It opens with a description of where the narrator is standing, and what his senses perceive. He hears noting but "the rivulet on from the lawn / Running down to my own dark wood". A rivulet is a little stream, which here runs from Maud's property to the narrator's house. The wood is dark, because it symbolizes the narrator's own depressed and black mood, and his own gloomy house. This contrasts with the light, represented by Maud. This is also an example of the pathetic fallacy, in which nature expresses the emotions of the narrator.

This use of nature imagery – and the pathetic fallacy - to express the narrator's inner turmoil continues. The narrator hears the sea, and it has a "voice", which is a use of personification, as if nature itself is speaking to the poet. There is a use of enjambment in the line: "the voice of the long sea-wave as it swell'd / Now and then in the dim-gray dawn", which carries the sense over two lines, the verse here echoing the long sound of the waves and their retreat. This is a mournful sound, and the waves of the sea have been described earlier in the poem (section three) in similarly eerie terms: "the scream of a madden'd beach dragg'd down by the wave".

All around the house, the curtains are being drawn to allow everyone to go to sleep. However, mention of an everyday image like a curtain becomes very sinister by the use of a compound adjective of "death-white". This means like a corpse, without life. The narrator is extremely affected by this, and he uses very physical imagery. A horror creeps over him, which will "prickle" his skin, as if he is afflicted by pins and needles.

The last two lines, as in the second stanza, become very long, with the final line up to fourteen syllables, as the narrator becomes increasingly agitated at his morbid imaginings. His rational mind sees that the "death-white curtain" being drawn simply means that it is early, and most people are asleep in the house, but his imagination sees something sinister: "I shudder'd and thought like a fool of the sleep of death". The linkage of sleep and death is an old image in English literature, with many examples (one of the most famous being from Shakespeare's *The Tempest*, when Prospero says that "our little life / Is rounded with a sleep"). Here, we see that the narrator is obsessed by death, finding images of it even when it is not there.

# XV

SO dark a mind within me dwells,
  And I make myself such evil cheer,
That if *I* be dear to some one else
  Then some one else may have much to fear;        *530*
But if *I* be dear to some one else,
  Then I should be to myself more dear.
Shall I not take care of all that I think,
Yea ev'n of wretched meat and drink,
If I be dear,                                       *535*
If I be dear to some one else.

Synopsis

The narrator, in a dark mood, tells himself that if he is indeed loved by someone else (Maud) that he should take better care of himself. However, he also says that if someone else does love him, that person might be in danger.

Verse Form

Section fifteen is a very short, self-contained section. The verse here is regular, mainly iambic (composed of feet of two syllables, unstressed followed by stressed), with the occasional additional syllable. Lines have around seven to eight syllables. This regularity of stress, and the initial four lines rhyming ABAB, show the narrator reflecting soberly on his dark moods, employing his reason, rather than his emotion. The penultimate line, however, is incredibly short – four syllables – and this shows the narrator pausing to let the weight of his reflections sink in.

Stanza 1

This very short stanza uses some very interesting techniques to express some very difficult ideas, in spite of its seeming simplicity. Firstly, it talks of a "dark" mind which "dwells" within the narrator. This points towards an idea that the narrator has an unconscious part of himself, over which his conscious, rational mind has no control. This is an idea which would be taken up later in the 19th century by such figures as the controversial psychoanalyst Sigmund Freud, who sought to understand mental illness by examining the hidden feelings and desires of people. Tennyson's interest here is not to propose a psychological theory, but to show that the narrator is aware that he cannot control his own dark feelings, which might overwhelm the narrator.

The narrator makes himself "evil cheer", which is an odd expression; in old English, the correct phrase would be "good cheer"; the use of "evil cheer" is unexpected and powerful and shows how the narrator is torturing himself, by dwelling on the morbid and evil sides of life. Because he is torturing himself, the narrator realizes that he is a danger to his loved ones. The way the narrator discusses this is interesting; he does not use the usual word "someone", but divides it into two words, "some one", which is not strictly correct. He says that "if *I* be dear to some one else / Then some one else may have much to fear". The use of italics for "*I*" emphasizes this word, and by using "some one" instead of "someone" the stress moved to "one" instead of the word "some". This surprising inversion of stress makes us aware who the "one" person is who could move the narrator so much: it is Maud herself.

The narrator realizes that he has to change his ways, to avoid harm to Maud and to himself. He repeats much of lines three to four, in lines five to six: "But if I be dear to some one else, / Then I should be to myself more dear". This means he needs to take better care of himself, even down to caring more for his physical needs, as well as his emotional needs: "Shall I not take care of all that I think, / Yea ev'n of wretched meat and drink". The word "wretched" shows the narrator's state of mind leaking out again; even normal, everyday things like food and drink are tainted and made wretched by his dark state of mind.

The final two lines both start with "if", making four instances of the word "if" in the whole section. This shows how the narrator continues to be uncertain about everything, including Maud's love. The penultimate line is very short, and implies a gap or pause after the four syllables; this gap expresses the strong doubt that the narrator feels about absolutely everything in his life. The final line, "If I be dear to some one else", leaves the reader, like the narrator, unresolved about whether Maud's love is genuine.

XVI

1

THIS lump of earth has left his estate
The lighter by the loss of his weight;
And so that he find what he went to seek,
And fulsome Pleasure clog him, and drown          *540*
His heart in the gross mud-honey of town,
He may stay for a year who has gone for a week.
But this is the day when I must speak,
And I see my Oread coming down,
O this is the day!                                *545*
O beautiful creature, what am I
That I dare to look her way;
Think I may hold dominion sweet,
Lord of the pulse that is lord of her breast,
And dream of her beauty with tender dread,        *550*
From the delicate Arab arch of her feet
To the grace that, bright and light as the crest
Of a peacock, sits on her shining head,
And she knows it not: O, if she knew it,
To know her beauty might half undo it.            *555*
I know it the one bright thing to save
My yet young life in the wilds of Time,
Perhaps from madness, perhaps from crime,
Perhaps from a selfish grave.

2                                  *560*

What, if she be fasten'd to this fool lord,
Dare I bid her abide by her word?
Should I love her so well if she
Had given her word to a thing so low?
Shall I love her as well if she
Can break her word were it even for me?           *565*
I trust that it is not so.

3

Catch not my breath, O clamorous heart,
Let not my tongue be a thrall to my eye
For I must tell her before we part,
I must tell her, or die.                          *570*

Synopsis

Maud's brother is away, and the narrator decides the time is right to declare his love to Maud openly.

Verse Form

Section six is composed of three irregular stanzas; most lines have four stresses and eight to nine syllables, but moments of heightened emotions lead to shorter lines (as in "O this is the day!", line 545). The first stanza – which dwells at length firstly on Maud's brother, then on Maud's beauty, is followed by two short stanzas, which are focused on inner struggle, over Maud's moral worthiness, and the narrator's own inability to act.

Stanzas 1 – 3

The first stanza is dominated firstly by images about the brother. He has left town. The first metaphor used describes him as a "lump of earth". This means he is heavy, like a piece of soil, contrasting him with the light, spiritual Maud. By calling him a lump of earth, it also emphasizes the brother's low, unpleasant and stupid qualities. The narrator goes on to wish the brother would remain away for a long time. He uses personification, as the brother's desire for fast living is introduced as the character "fulsome Pleasure", which might "clog him" and "drown him" in the "gross mud-honey of town". This means the brother might eat and drink so much that the he chooses to stay in London. The compound word "mud-honey" means that what seems sweet might quickly become cloying, like an addict who starts with something pleasant and seemingly harmless but then cannot stop.

The narrator knows that he can seek his chance to declare his love when the brother is away, "this is the day when I must speak". The narrator uses a reference to ancient Greek mythology to describe Maud. She is described as an Oread, which is a mountain-nymph, or beautiful imaginary creature. This airy spirit of the mountains is a contrast to the earth-bound brother, mired in the mud of the town. The narrator then lets his emotions break out in two lines which begin with "O", showing he cannot contain his joy. The very short line "O this is the day!" is followed immediately and characteristically by a hesitation and sense of self-doubt. The narrator asks "What am I / That I dare to look her way", the startling enjambment emphasizing his sense of worthlessness.

He questions whether he will ever hold "dominion sweet" over her emotions, and be "Lord" of her heart. The use of these words of power and conquest – "dominion" and "Lord" show that the narrator sees love between men and women as one of dominance, which is a common way that men thought about gender relations in the 19th century.

Maud's power over the narrator can still unsettle him; he thinks of her beauty with "tender dread". He returns to the imagery of the *Arabian Nights* here, as in earlier sections, to give Maud's beauty a sense of the exotic. He describes her feet as a "delicate Arab arch", which is an image taken from architecture. Arches were particular beautiful and delicate in the Islamic world; famous examples are found in the beautiful Alahambra palace in southern Spain. This architecture combines strength with beauty, and a sense of airiness. He also talks of "grace" sitting on her "bright and light as the crest / Of a peacock". These images of lightness contrast again with the earthiness of her brother.

The narrator then says that Maud is unaware of her own beauty, a modesty which adds to her charm. There is a rare use of a feminine rhyme here in "knew it" and "undo it", which emphasizes further the importance of modesty to the narrator. But in talking about her beauty, he introduces a note of darkness. She is the "one bright thing" which can rescue the narrator from the "wilds of Time". He then piles up sinister image after sinister image, in "madness", "crime" and a "selfish grave". We are aware of her vital importance to the narrator's mental health.

In the second stanza, the narrator again hesitates: can he trust Maud if she has said yes to the new made-lord? Does this mean he can never love her again? Then, he wonders if Maud did say yes and break off her engagement, is this proof of her fickleness, and does that make her less worthy? This shows an obsession with Maud's virtue which is typical in the Victorian era, in which the purity and morality of woman became an overriding concern of men.

The final stanza shows the narrator realizing he must act. He tries to give himself courage, and talks to his own "clamorous heart", telling his "tongue" not to "be a thrall to my eye", meaning he hopes the sight of Maud's beauty won't make him lose his nerve. His final line makes it clear that his love for Maud is a literally a matter of life and death: "I must tell her, or die". The reader sees that, as elsewhere in *Maud*, love and death and never far apart.

XVII

GO not, happy day,
  From the shining fields,
Go not, happy day,
  Till the maiden yields.
Rosy is the West,                      *575*
  Rosy is the South,
Roses are her cheeks,
  And a rose her mouth.
When the happy Yes
  Falters from her lips,               *580*
Pass and blush the news
  O'er the blowing ships.
Over blowing seas,
  Over seas at rest,
Pass the happy news,                   *585*
  Blush it thro' the West;
Till the red man dance
  By his red cedar tree,
And the red man's babe
  Leap, beyond the sea.                *590*
Blush from West to East,
  Blush from East to West,
Till the West is East,
  Blush it thro' the West.
Rosy is the West,                      *595*
  Rosy is the South,
Roses are her cheeks,
  And a rose her mouth.

Synopsis

The narrator is about to declare his love to Maud. He imagines her saying yes, and in his fantasy seems to see the whole world rejoicing at the fact.

Verse Form

Section seventeen is composed of one long stanza of twenty-eight lines – essentially seven groups of four lines, rhyming ABCB. There is a very strong rhythm, which uses a rare "trochaic" metre (stressed, then unstressed, with an extra stress syllable, making a five-syllable line). This gives a powerful musical effect, as if a drum were being banged, or as if the narrator is being pulled forward by the momentum of his passion.

Stanza 1

This whole stanza contains some of the most troubling lines and concepts in *Maud* for a modern reader. It opens with a poetic address to the "happy day", who is told by the narrator not to go "from the shining fields". We have moved a long way from the narrator's usual darkness. However, the next lines are more problematic. The narrator is asking for the happy day to stay "Till the maiden yields". This sees the relationship of narrator and Maud not as equals, but again as a battle in which he will seek to overcome her and make her surrender to him. It picks up the unpleasant thought of trying to establish "dominion" over Maud from the previous stanza, and reinforces a sense that the narrator is unable to consider Maud outside of the usual chauvinistic 19th century views of gender relations.

Lines four to eight pick up the rose imagery used earlier in *Maud*; we have seen how the rose can symbolize passion,; here it is used in an image of sunset in the south and the west, as the day is closing: "Rosy is the West, / Rosy is the South". The whole world seems to be responding to Maud's beauty, which is also now described in images which are red in colour: "Rosy are her cheeks, / And a rose her mouth". But the colour red, especially in connection with a mouth, is not always positive in Maud; it is often very negative. The opening lines of the whole poem – which describe the hollow where Maud's father died – used red lips to symbolize death and blood: "lips in the field above are dabbled with blood-red heath". We cannot read the description of a rosy mouth as positively as the narrator is trying to do so; we always remember that red is a colour of blood and death. The red mouth is also a deeply sexual image; her "rosy cheeks" could be read as sexual arousal, and the "rosy mouth" as Maud's vagina, which could never be mentioned in a poem from the 19th century, but could be alluded to in such a cryptic image.

The next few lines move to the narrator's fantasy that Maud will return his love. A "happy yes / Falters from her lips". "Falters" however implies that Maud may be initially unwilling. But the narrator glosses over that. The narrator's excitement causes him to brush away Maud's hesitation in imagine fantastical images: news of their love will travel to all corners of the world, the "blowing ships" over the "blowing seas" carrying the good tidings.

At this point, the narrator imagines that, far in the West, Native Americans will celebrate the good tidings. The language used by Tennyson to describe the Native Americans is no longer politically acceptable. Native Americans – once wrongly called American Indians – are the original first peoples of the Americas, who had been oppressed by European settlers, killed in their masses and driven from their ancestral homes. The narrator calls these people "the red man" – now a racial slur. He imagines them dancing for joy at news of Maud saying "yes". This image is not only offensive to our eyes, but absurd even to contemporaries, and the 19th century reader at this point would perhaps recognize that the narrator is becoming carried away, and the imagery is deliberately ridiculous. When the narrator uses an image of a Native American child leaping for joy across the sea, we might read this as Tennyson signaling the narrator is losing touch with reality, as he is lost in his imagination, and his potential joy.

(In 1855, the same year as *Maud* was published, Henry Longfellow published his famous poem *Hiawatha*, about Native Americans; this is also in trochaic verse. This use of the strong, unusual beat of trochaic rhythm in both poems is meant to give an exotic sense of strangeness, and echo the supposed rhythm of Native American drums.)

The narrator imagines the whole world turning red from the news of Maud saying yes: "Blush from West to East, / Blush from East to West, / Till the West is East, / Blush it thro' the West." The narrator then returns, from these overblown fantasies, to Maud once more, repeating lines five to eight again, ending with the image of Maud's rosy mouth – here, as mentioned earlier, a powerfully erotic image.

## XVIII

### 1

I HAVE led her home, my love, my only friend.
There is none like her, none.                          *600*
And never yet so warmly ran my blood
And sweetly, on and on
Calming itself to the long-wish'd-for end,
Full to the banks, close on the promised good.

                                                        *605*
### 2

None like her, none.
Just now the dry-tongued laurel's pattering talk
Seem'd her light foot along the garden walk,
And shook my heart to think she comes once more,
But even then I heard her close the door,
The gates of Heaven are closed, and she is gone.       *610*

### 3

There is none like her, none.
Nor will be when our summers have deceased.
O, art thou sighing for Lebanon
In the long breeze that streams to thy delicious East,
Sighing for Lebanon,                                   *615*
Dark cedar, tho' thy limbs have here increased,
Upon a pastoral slope as fair,
And looking to the South, and fed
With honey'd rain and delicate air,
And haunted by the starry head                         *620*
Of her whose gentle will has changed my fate,
And made my life a perfumed altar-flame;
And over whom thy darkness must have spread
With such delight as theirs of old, thy great
Forefathers of the thornless garden, there             *625*
Shadowing the snow-limb'd Eve from whom she came.

Synopsis

Section eighteen opens after the narrator has declared his love to Maud, who has reciprocated in kissing him. The narrator has walked her home, and on leaving her in her garden, he imagines what the cedar tree in her garden has seen.

Verse Form

Section eighteen is composed of eight very irregular stanzas, in which lines of up to twelve syllables are balanced by very short refrains. Much use of archaic vocabulary and repetition of "and" at the start of lines gives the section the feel of Biblical verse, from the Old Testament especially. This suits the theme of the everlasting nature of Maud's love, and its overwhelming spiritual and physical importance to the narrator.

Stanza 1-3

The first short stanza sets the scene; the narrator has led Maud back home. She is the narrators "only friend", his "love". The second line, "There is none like her, none", is repeated at the start of stanzas two and three, linking the stanzas together into a declaration of love for Maud. The rest of stanza one is taken up by a metaphor; the narrator likens his blood to a river, which has risen "Full to the banks" but is now "Calming itself to the long-wish'd-for end". This means that the river in flood is now dying down; in terms of the narrator's love, this means that the violent emotion of his love is more peaceful now that Maud has returned his love.

The second stanza is similar in structure to the first; again, six lines, with the repeated short line of "None like her, none" opening it. The narrator then introduces an image of nature. The sound of the laurel leaves in the wind sounds like Maud's feet on the garden path. The word "pattering" here is an example of onomatopoeia, as it mimics the sounds of the rustling leaves. The laurel tree is personified, with words like "dry-tongued" and "talk" seemingly giving the trees a human character. The narrator is violently agitated to think that Maud might be returning: he says it "shook my heart to think she comes once more". But she is actually only closing the door to her house. There is a use of hyperbole or overstatement here, when the door to Maud's house is described as the "gates of Heaven"; this overstatement shows how important Maud is to the narrator.

The third, longer stanza picks up a Biblical theme, as hinted at in "gates of Heaven", and develops this in relation to the idea of nature being personified. The central image in this section is a cedar tree, more specifically a cedar of Lebanon, which is a country in the Middle East near Israel. This passage resembles in structure and imagery a specific book of the Old Testament – the *Song of Songs* or *Song of Solomon*, which has been seen as a celebration of sexual love. It also mentions Lebanon in relation to the beloved, and the beauties of the natural world.

The stanza opens with the repeated "There is none like her, none", and continues to say that Maud will remain unique even after she and the narrator are dead: "when our summers have deceased". The poem then begins to address the cedar tree in Maud's garden directly. The narrator asks whether the tree is "sighing for Lebanon / In the long breeze that streams to this delicious East". The length of this line – twelve syllables – echoes the sense of the slow breeze moving eastwards. Again, a short line breaks this thought: "Sighing for Lebanon", repeating the end of the third line. This is a very artificial and poetic language, which sounds musical, exotic, and biblical.

Although the cedar might be sighing for its home, England's "pastoral slope" has allowed the cedar to grow, due to its "honey'd rain and delicate air". The tree, like the narrator, though is "haunted" by Maud. This odd use of the word in such an otherwise positive stanza points forward to the hauntings of part two of *Maud*.

The narrator's "fate" has been changed by Maud, and has made his life a "perfumed altar-flame". Again, this is a use of exotic religious language to describe passion. It means that the narrator has sacrificed his life to Maud. The stanza ends with another biblical image, as he imagines the cedar's ancestors giving shade in the Garden of Eden to Maud's ancestor – the "snow-limb'd Eve". However, there are two ominous notes here. Describing the garden as "thornless" echoes another biblical use of thorns – the crown of thorns on Christ's head. Death therefore enters the garden. And 19th century readers would know that to mention Eve means remembering the other part of the Garden of Eden story: that Eve's eating of the fruit of the tree of knowledge would lead to the banishing of her, Adam, and all mankind from paradise. Maud may be the narrator's love, but, like Eve, will she ultimately prove harmful?

4

Here will I lie, while these long branches sway,
And you fair stars that crown a happy day
Go in and out as if at merry play,
Who am no more so all forlorn                                    *630*
As when it seem'd far better to be born
To labour and the mattock-harden'd hand,
Than nursed at ease and brought to understand
A sad astrology, the boundless plan                              *635*
That makes you tyrants in your iron skies,
Innumerable, pitiless, passionless eyes,
Cold fires, yet with power to burn and brand
His nothingness into man.

5

But now shine on, and what care I,
Who in this stormy gulf have found a pearl                       *640*
The countercharm of space and hollow sky,
And do accept my madness, and would die
To save from some slight shame one simple girl.

6

Would die; for sullen-seeming Death may give
More life to love than is or ever was                            *645*
In our low world, where yet 'tis sweet to live.
Let no one ask me how it came to pass;
It seems that I am happy, that to me
A livelier emerald twinkles in the grass,
A purer sapphire melts into the sea.                             *650*

7

Not die; but live a life of truest breath,
And teach true life to fight with mortal wrongs.
O, why should Love, like men in drinking-songs,
Spice his fair banquet with the dust of death?
Make answer, Maud my bliss,                                      *655*
Maud made my Maud by that long loving kiss,
Life of my life, wilt thou not answer this?
"The dusky strand of Death inwoven here
With dear Love's tie, makes Love himself more dear."

Synopsis

The narrator addresses the stars above. He says that, in the past, he regarded them as sinister, emblematic of an uncaring universe. Now Maud has accepted his love, he no longer finds them threatening. The narrator loves her so much he pledges he would die for her; he thinks at length about the close tie between love and death.

Stanzas 4 -7

The opening of stanza four is playful and serene; the narrator lying beneath the cedar tree. The first three lines of stanza all rhyme, with "branches sway", "happy day" and "merry play" setting a calm scene. The "fair stars", though, set the narrator off on a typical train of thought, moving jarringly from the happy present to describe how he felt in the past, before meeting Maud. Then, the narrator was "forlorn" or sad. He would have preferred to have been born a peasant, without any understanding of the true nature of the world. He wished he had been "born / To labour and the mattock-hardn'd hand", a mattock being a farming tool. Unfortunately, being educated means he understands too much of the modern "sad astrology" of the stars. This means the narrator understands modern science, which has replaced comforting old beliefs with a godless mechanical universe. Under old astrology, the constellations ruled man's fate. But now the stars are only "tyrants" in their "iron skies", ruled by physics, predictable in their courses. The stars are "Innumerable, pitiless, passionless", merely "Cold fires". They only have the paradoxical power to "burn and brand" a sense of "nothingness" into mankind. This image is an oxymoron, or contradiction in terms, as fires cannot be cold; it shows us how unnatural the narrator felt in his loneliness, and how he was himself cold and lacking in emotion.

The narrator in stanza five, though, is saved from this sense of nothingness by Maud. He describes her using the metaphor of a pearl, which is precious and rare. She is the "countercharm of space and hollow sky", which means the magic of her love saves the narrator from his loneliness. She also accepts "his madness". The narrator's possible madness has been beneath the surface of the poem to date, always threatening. The narrator then introduces the next theme of this section: the linking of love with death. The narrator is willing to "die / To save from some slight shame one simple girl.' The use of sibilance here shows the strength of the narrator's emotion.

The next stanza develops the narrator's morbid preoccupation for dying for Maud; he opens with a repetition from the last stanza, in "Would die", which seems odd with no subject "I" in front of the verb. He says that "sullen-seeming Death may give / More life to love than is or ever was". However, the narrator admits that "yet 'tis sweet to live", though he is still partly confused as to why he is so content: "It seems that I am happy" shows the narrator bemused at the effect Maud's love has had. As Maud has been described as a jewel many times in the poem, so her presence causes the narrator to use jewel imagery to show the natural world. A "livelier emerald" is in the green of the grass, and "A purer sapphire" is in the blue of the sea. This shows how love of Maud improves all he sees.

Stanza seven though circles back to death; here the narrator opens with a defiant choice of live: "Not die; but live a life of truest breath". He cannot escape from a sense that the thought of death gives a greater meaning to love, or that love is never free from the threat of death. He asks a question to Maud: "O, why should Love, like men in drinking-songs, / Spice his fair banquet with the dust of death?" This image is very complicated, but seems to mean that the "fair banquet" of love is always going to be destroyed by death. All lovers will eventually age and die. This awareness of death actually should make us aware how fragile love is, and not waste it when it arrives. Much art in the 19th century covered this theme, as life expectancy was much lower, and infant mortality rates very high; people lived much more closely with death than we do in the 21st century, and Tennyson himself had been deeply scarred by the death in 1833 of his closest friend Arthur Hallam.

The narrator insists on Maud answering his question (although this is of course just in his imagination, as Maud has gone inside). He asks her in imagination to "Make answer, Maud my bliss". We now learn that she has returned his love physically, "Maud made my Maud by that long loving kiss". The "m" and "d" sounds at the start of the line are almost a tongue-twister, and again show the narrator's obsession with her. The final two lines of the stanza are in quotation marks, and are another challenge for Maud to answer: "The dusky strand of Death inwoven here / With dear Love's tie, makes Love himself more dear". This does not seem to be a citation from another author, in spite of the quotation marks. The metaphor is taken from cloth-making; a dark strand (representing death) has been woven into the fabric (representing love) and this makes it more attractive. This means that the thought of death makes love more precious.

Is that enchanted moan only the swell
Of the long waves that roll in yonder bay?
And hark the clock within, the silver knell
Of twelve sweet hours that past in bridal white,
And died to live, long as my pulses play;
But now by this my love has closed her sight *665*
And given false death her hand, and stol'n away
To dreamful wastes where footless fancies dwell
Among the fragments of the golden day.
May nothing there her maiden grace affright!
Dear heart, I feel with thee the drowsy spell. *670*
My bride to be, my evermore delight,
My own heart's heart, my ownest own, farewell;
It is but for a little space I go:
And ye meanwhile far over moor and fell
Beat to the noiseless music of the night! *675*
Has our whole earth gone nearer to the glow
Of your soft splendours that you look so bright?
*I* have climb'd nearer out of lonely Hell.
Beat, happy stars, timing with things below,
Beat with my heart more blest than heart can tell, *680*
Blest, but for some dark undercurrent woe
That seems to draw—but it shall not be so:
Let all be well, be well.

Synopsis

The narrator makes his way home after hearing the clock in Maud's house chime midnight. He imagines the whole of nature beating along with the rhythm of his own heart. He feels for once in sympathy with the universe. However, he ends this section with a premonition of disaster, which he tries to ignore.

Stanza 8

The whole stanza, which takes as its central metaphor the narrator's heartbeat, cleverly uses very few rhymes across its 24 line length. Two main rhyme sounds dominate: the words "swell", "knell", "dwell", "spell", "farewell", "fell", "Hell", "tell" and "well" (the latter repeated), and the words "white", "sight", "affright", "delight", "night" and "bright". The close alternation of these rhymes sounds like a heartbeat itself.

The stanza opens with the sound of the sea once more. Throughout *Maud* the sound of the sea is either sinister or comforting, depending on the narrator's underlying mood. Here, it is positive, an "enchanted moan", picking up the imagery of Maud as magical "countercharm" against sadness. The narrator hears the clock, which has struck midnight, "the silver knell / Of twelve sweet hours that past in bridal white". This is a curious image, and seems to mean that the narrator has spent all day with Maud, imagining she will be his bride. The day has "died to live long as my pulses play". This is another difficult image, and seems to allude to an old-fashioned expression that sees nightfall as the dying of the day; again, we see that the narrator finds it difficult to keep his mind away from death even when he is in the middle of his happiest moment. The introduction of "pulses play" prepares us for the metaphor of the narrator's heart beating in sympathy with nature that dominates the second half of the stanza.

The narrator then imagines Maud asleep with her eyes closed. But again, the narrator returns to thoughts of death: Maud has "given false death her hand". This means on one level she has just fallen asleep – but to give one's hand means to marry. Does this mean that she has somehow married death? The narrator is quick to move on from this troubling image, to more positive and fanciful ones of Maud's dreams, where "footless fancies dwell / Among the fragments of the golden day". The "f" alliterations are meant here to be musical and soothing. The word "footless" means insubstantial or airy; the implication is these are good dreams, recollections of the joyful day just spent. Indeed, the narrator wishes her sweet dreams, with nothing to "affright" or scare her.

The next few lines are wholly positive, and develop the heartbeat theme of this stanza. He calls Maud his "Dear heart", his "own heart's heart" and his "ownest own". The last of these, using a very odd but effective superlative, draws attention to how closely he feels to Maud, and how he feels she is now almost a part of him.

In the next few lines, the narrator's imagines Maud, far from him, "over moor and fell". He speaks to her heart, asking it to "Beat to the noiseless music of the night". The natural world is in sympathy with Maud, the "whole earth gone nearer / To the glow of your soft splendours".

The narrator has been rescued from his misery by Maud, climbing "out of lonely Hell". He picks up the word "beat" and starts the next two lines with this word, further echoing his heartbeat. The stars, which in stanza four were "pitiless […] Cold fires", are now happy; the narrator asks them to show this happiness: "Beat, happy stars, timing with things below / Beat with my heart, more blest than heart can tell". However, this universal happiness does not last. The narrator cannot help but show his anxiety in the next lines: "Blest, but for some dark undercurrent woe / That seems to draw – but it shall not be so". The word "undercurrent" is a metaphor of being dragged under water by a powerful tide. This means that the narrator could be dragged down by his own depression, or by fate. Tennyson uses ellipsis here to show the narrator's anxiety: the narrator doesn't finish his sentence, leaving the word "draw" dangling. The narrator very quickly shuts down this morbid train of the thought. The stanza finishes with a plea, which is almost a prayer: "Let all be well, be well". However, the reader must be uneasy: this "dark undercurrent" and the narrator's unfinished expression of dread foreshadow an impending tragedy in the poem.

# XIX

## 1

HER brother is coming back to-night,                    *685*
Breaking up my dream of delight.

## 2

My dream? do I dream of bliss?
I have walk'd awake with Truth.
O when did a morning shine
So rich in atonement as this
For my dark-dawning youth,                              *690*
Darken'd watching a mother decline
And that dead man at her heart and mine:
For who was left to watch her but I?
Yet so did I let my freshness die.

## 3                                                     *695*

I trust that I did not talk
To gentle Maud in our walk
(For often in lonely wanderings
I have cursed him even to lifeless things)
But I trust that I did not talk,
Not touch on her father's sin:                          *700*
I am sure I did but speak
Of my mother's faded cheek
When it slowly grew so thin,
That I felt she was slowly dying
Vext with lawyers and harass'd with debt:               *705*
For how often I caught her with eyes all wet,
Shaking her head at her son and sighing,
A world of trouble within!

Synopsis

The narrator realizes that the return of Maud's brother might signal the end of their relationship. The narrator tells of the death of his mother.

Verse Form

Section nineteen, typically for *Maud*, alternates very short stanzas (two lines) with much longer verses (eighteen lines). After the long, biblically-inspired lines of section eighteen, this section – devoted to less fantastic thoughts – has short lines, typically conversational in tone. The narrator grapples with memory of the past, coming to terms with having a normal relationship with Maud and her untrustworthy brother.

Throughout this section, there are many rhyming couplets; these are used by Tennyson to show the narrator struggling to bring regularity and order to his thinking, and establish control over himself.

Stanzas 1-3

Stanza one is extremely short – two lines, a rhyming couplet – which uses one of the two main rhymes of the closing stanza of section eighteen: "Her brother is coming back to-night / Breaking up my dream of delight". The ironic re-use of the "ight" sound here shows how the narrator's happiness was very short-lived, only a "dream". However, typical of the contradictions of the narrator's argument, stanza two immediately corrects this. It was not a "dream of bliss"; "I have walk'd awake with Truth". The narrator is trying very hard to convince himself of his good fortune.

The rest of stanza two introduces the narrator's mother. Maud's love is "atonement", or a making of amends for the wrongs the narrator had to undergo. The use of the "d" sound in the rest of the stanza links everything to death, one of Maud's key themes, and the closing image of the stanza. The narrator's youth was "dark-dawning", because it was "Darken'd watching a mother decline / And that dead man at her heart and mine". Her mother died haunted by the memory of her husband, ruined by Maud's father. The narrator was left alone to look after his mother, which has marked him profoundly: "Yet so did I let my freshness die". The word "die", rhyming with "I", links the narrator with death itself. The narrator's "freshness" or youth has been destroyed by his parents' death.

Stanza three opens with the narrator worried he did not ruin things with Maud by telling her about her "father's sin" – namely, her father's role in ruining the narrator's father, and causing his suicide. The narrator hints here that he has been unable to control his emotions: "For often in lonely wanderings / I have cursed him even to lifeless things". This means that he has made outbursts even when no-one else was there. The narrator attempts to reassure himself that he "did but speak / Of my mother's faded cheek", rather than rage at her father. But he, and the reader, cannot be sure that he didn't.

The narrator paints a very vivid picture of his mother in her last days, "slowly dying / Vext with lawyers and harass'd with debt". The narrator's mother main object of worry was her son; he caught her often "with eyes all wet / Shaking her head at her son and sighing". The sibilance of "s" here in this line creates an effect of the sound of her sighing. The final line, with an exclamation mark at the end for added emphasis, shows how strongly the mother feels her son has been affected: "A world of trouble within!"

4

And Maud too, Maud was moved
To speak of the mother she loved                    *710*
As one scarce less forlorn,
Dying abroad and it seems apart
From him who had ceased to share her heart,
And ever mourning over the feud,
The household Fury sprinkled with blood             *715*
By which our houses are torn:
How strange was what she said,
When only Maud and the brother
Hung over her dying bed—
That Maud's dark father and mine                    *720*
Had bound us one to the other,
Betrothed us over their wine,
On the day when Maud was born;
Seal'd her mine from her first sweet breath.
Mine, mine by a right, from birth till death        *725*
Mine, mine—our fathers have sworn.

5

But the true blood spilt had in it a heat
To dissolve the precious seal on a bond,
That, if left uncancell'd, had been so sweet:
And none of us thought of a something beyond,       *730*
A desire that awoke in the heart of the child,
As it were a duty done to the tomb,
To be friends for her sake, to be reconciled;
And I was cursing them and my doom,
And letting a dangerous thought run wild            *735*
While often abroad in the fragrant gloom
Of foreign churches—I see her there,
Bright English lily, breathing a prayer
To be friends, to be reconciled!

Synopsis

Maud told the narrator about her mother's death. Maud's mother died abroad, estranged from Maud's father. On her deathbed, Maud's mother told Maud and her brother about the abandoned plan to betroth Maud to the narrator. While the narrator had not been aware of this plan, Maud, throughout her childhood abroad, had prayed to be reconciled to him.

Stanzas 4-5

Stanzas four and five are primarily narrative, and fill in details of the plot. Stanza four opens with Maud discussing her own mother: "And Maud too, Maud was moved / To speak of the mother she loved". This is an "eye-rhyme" only, as moved and loved are pronounced differently. In *Maud* such eye-rhymes usually signal emotional distress – here, Maud remembering her mother, who is "scarce less forlorn" than the narrator's. Maud's mother died abroad, estranged from her husband, and devastated by the actions of her husband which had torn both families apart. This is described as "the feud / The household Fury sprinkled with blood / By which our houses are torn". The word "Fury" here relates to figures from ancient Greek mythology. A Fury was a goddess of vengeance; they were known as "The Kindly Ones" or the Eumenides, as to mention their real names was bad luck. To mention the Furies here acknowledges that the terrible outcome of her life, and her family's exile, was punishment for her husband's sins.

On her deathbed, Maud's mother admitted the story which was hinted at in the mysterious section seven of *Maud*, when the narrator remembered as if in a dream a pact that his father and Maud's father made. Here, the narrator says Maud's mother made it clear: "Maud's dark father and mine / Had bound us one to the other, / Betrothed us over their wine / On the day when Maud was born". (Here, we should note that section nineteen of *Maud* was only added to the second edition in 1856, because Tennyson realized that it was not clear enough that the narrator and Maud had been betrothed; section seven had been felt to be too obscure by early readers).

The last three lines of stanza four show the narrator's reaction to this news; she was "mine from her first sweet breath. / Mine, mine by a right, from birth till death / Mine, mine – our fathers have sworn". This is another example of the narrator seeing Maud as a possession; he repeats the word "mine" five times in a frenzy; he considers Maud his, because their fathers decided it. Like many women in the 19th century, Maud seems like an object, her future love and marriage set by her parents, without her having any say in the matter.

The next stanza opens with an image from the law; the "bond" or contract between the families has been dissolved – the "true blood spilt" in the death of the narrator's father had in effect rendered the arrangement between Maud and the narrator cancelled. If it had been allowed, it "had been so sweet", the narrator says, echoing the numerous other times in the poem when "sweet" is used to describe Maud's love. However, her mother's dying words affected Maud, something "awoke in the heart of the child, / As it were a duty done to the tomb". She will work towards a reconciliation between herself and the narrator.

While the narrator was sunk in his depression and suicidal thoughts, Maud was praying for him. The narrator uses a very striking image of Maud "in the fragrant gloom of foreign churches", "fragrant" because they are presumably Roman Catholic, incense being less common in Protestant churches. The narrator calls her a "Bright English lily" as she prays "To be friends, to be reconciled".

The use of the imagery of the lily, as mentioned earlier, contrasts with use of the imagery of the rose in *Maud*. The lily means purity and virginity; when the narrator uses rose imagery, it is usually in connection with erotic love and death. Therefore the narrator here sees Maud in very religious terms. The lily is the flower most strongly associated with the Virgin Mary, the mother of Christ. The two loving and idealized mothers (the narrator's and Maud's) and Mary, the perfect mother, all provide an alternative to the influence of fathers. Fathers in *Maud* are usually negative (the narrator's father's bankruptcy, madness and suicide, and Maud's father's corruption and tyranny).

But then what a flint is he!
Abroad, at Florence, at Rome,
I find whenever she touch'd on me
This brother had laugh'd her down,
And at last, when each came home,                    *745*
He had darken'd into a frown,
Chid her, and forbid her to speak
To me, her friend of the years before;
And this was what had redden'd her cheek
When I bow'd to her on the moor.

Yet Maud, altho' not blind
To the faults of his heart and mind,
I see she cannot but love him,
And says he is rough but kind,
And wishes me to approve him,
And tells me, when she lay                           *755*
Sick once, with a fear of worse,
That he left his wine and horses and play,
Sat with her, read to her, night and day,
And tended her like a nurse.

Kind? but the deathbed desire
Spurn'd by this heir of the liar—
Rough but kind? yet I know
He has plotted against me in this,
That he plots against me still.
Kind to Maud? that were not amiss.                   *765*
Well, rough but kind; why, let it be so:
For shall not Maud have her will?

Synopsis

The narrator learns that Maud's brother had forbidden her to speak to him, which explains her cold behaviour when they met again recently. The narrator agrees to be polite to the brother, for Maud's sake.

Stanza 6 – 8

Stanza six picks up the image of stone to describe Maud's brother. This was used in section thirteen (a "stony British stare") in the same way; here, the brother is described as "flint". This image means that like the stone, he is hard and unyielding and cruel. A flint as well is used to create fire; this implies that the brother might be quick to anger.

We learn more in this stanza of Maud's "back story". While living abroad in Italy (Florence and Rome), whenever Maud mentioned the narrator, the brother either laughed at Maud, or "darken'd into a frown". This was the true cause of Maud's embarrassment and distress at meeting the narrator after so many years: "this was what had redden'd her cheek / When I bow'd to her on the moor". We see that first appearances cannot be trusted, as we do not know peoples' genuine motives. What appeared to the narrator as pride and arrogance was in fact the very opposite.

Stanza seven continues this theme that people may be other than they first appear; we see a very different side of the brother. The verse here is deliberately flat and prosaic; five of the ten lines start with "And", signaling this is just a stanza supplying information, which can be quite dull and monotonous. We learn that Maud is aware of her brother's faults, but loves him regardless, so she wants the narrator to at least "approve" of the brother. When Maud was sick, "with a fear of worse", perhaps on her deathbed, her brother "left his wine and horses and play", and nursed her back to heath, sitting and reading to her. The narrator uses the simile "like a nurse", to show how he could soften his usual selfish and emotionless exterior.

Stanza eight however, changes tone, after this very matter-of-fact description. The narrator's anger at the brother bursts out. The stanza opens with a single word as a question: "Kind?" An uncommon feminine rhyme and the harsh "d" alliteration express the narrator's disgust: "the deathbed desire / Spurn'd by the heir of this liar - / Rough but kind". The "liar" is Maud's father, who cheated the narrator out of his inheritance. The paranoia of the narrator about Maud's brother comes through: "I know / He has plotted against me in this, / That he plots against me still". But the narrator pulls himself up. The narrator admits that in nursing Maud, the brother did show genuine kindness. Maud wants a reconciliation, so the narrator will give in: "Well, rough but kind; why, let it be so: / For shall not Maud have her will?"

## 9

For, Maud, so tender and true,
As long as my life endures
I feel I shall owe you a debt,                          *770*
That I never can hope to pay;
And if ever I should forget
That I owe this debt to you
And for your sweet sake to yours;
O then, what then shall I say?—                         *775*
If ever I *should* forget,
May God make me more wretched
Than ever I have been yet!

## 10

So now I have sworn to bury
All this dead body of hate,                             *780*
I feel so free and so clear
By the loss of that dead weight,
That I should grow light-headed, I fear,
Fantastically merry;
But that her brother comes, like a blight              *785*
On my fresh hope, to the Hall to-night.

Synopsis

The narrator swears that he will put aside hatred of her brother for Maud's sake. He says this should make him feel happier, but the section closes with the narrator dreading the brother's arrival back at the hall.

Stanzas 9 – 10

Stanza nine uses as a central metaphor the idea that the narrator owes Maud a debt, for freeing him from his sadness and making him happy. Maud is described as "tender and true". The narrator says he will never be able to repay his debt to Maud, and if he ever forgets it, he should be cursed: "If ever I *should* forget, / May God make me more wretched / Than ever I have been yet!"

The use of the metaphor of being in debt returns us uneasily back to the very start of the poem, where we learn that the narrator's father died after being ruined financially by Maud's father: the narrator's father literally committed suicide because of this financial debt. Also, we have just learned that the narrator's mother died "harass'd by debt". To describe love of Maud in terms of debt reminds the reader of this fact. Like the narrator, can the reader trust Maud and her family, and can the narrator ever be free of resentment of his father's fate? Also, in the midst of his supposed happiness, the narrator uses the very strong word "wretched" to describe his potential fate. Again, misery is never far from the surface of *Maud*.

Aside from this hidden reference to his father's fate, the narrator in stanza ten uses another metaphor with a sinister double meaning. He describes his desire to forgive in very sinister terms: "I have sworn to bury / All this dead body of hate". By describing his animosity as a "dead body of fate", this reminds us of the image of the dead body of the narrator's father back in section one. The fourth line also introduces a very grim pun, calling his long-held resentment as "dead weight". The narrator should, by moving on from his feud, be feeling "light-headed" or "fantastically merry". However, he cannot escape from a feeling of dread. The final rhyming couplet echoes the opening lines of section nineteen: "But that he brother comes, like a blight / On my fresh hope, to the Hall to-night".

The word "blight" means a disease on crops or plants, which destroys them. This image means that the brother's presence will destroy the narrator's hopes. The strong, jarring enjambment between "blight / On my fresh hope" expresses the discord that the brother's presence will bring.

# XX

## 1

STRANGE, that I felt so gay,
Strange, that *I* tried to-day
To beguile her melancholy;
The Sultan, as we name him,—                    *790*
She did not wish to blame him—
But he vext her and perplext her
With his worldly talk and folly:
Was it gentle to reprove her
For stealing out of view                         *795*
From a little lazy lover
Who but claims her as his due?
Or for chilling his caresses
By the coldness of her manners,
Nay, the plainness of her dresses?               *800*
Now I know her but in two,
Nor can pronounce upon it
If one should ask me whether
The habit, hat, and feather,
Or the frock and gipsy bonnet                    *805*
Be the neater and completer;
For nothing can be sweeter
Than maiden Maud in either.

## 2

But to-morrow, if we live,
Our ponderous squire will give                   *810*
A grand political dinner
To half the squirelings near;
And Maud will wear her jewels,
And the bird of prey will hover,
And the titmouse hope to win her                 *815*
With his chirrup at her ear.

Synopsis

The narrator has been comforting Maud, who is upset because her brother has criticized her. Maud's brother reproved her for not spending enough time with her suitor, the new-made lord, and for the plainness of her clothes. The narrator says he loves Maud however she is dressed. Tomorrow night, Maud's brother is hosting a dinner for local gentry and his political supporters, and Maud is expected to dress up to impress the guests and her rich suitor.

Verse Form

Section twenty is composed of four stanzas of irregular length – from twenty-two lines to seven lines. Lines are short, at seven or eight syllables. The most remarkable feature of this section is the number of feminine or two-syllable rhymes: in stanza one the majority of rhymes are feminine, including internal rhymes. Feminine rhymes are rare in English verse, and the effect is usually seen as comic, or satirical. (The Irish satirical writer Jonathan Swift used feminine rhymes extensively, for example.) In this section, we can see much satire – or comic writing used for a serious moral end – about the brother's political ambitions and the new-made lord's attempts to woo Maud.

Stanzas 1-2

The stanza opens with the word "strange" repeated to open lines one and two; it is certainly strange to think of Maud as melancholy, and the narrator as consoling her sadness, given his history of depression. The first major note of satire, or criticism expressed with humour, enters in the description of Maud's brother as the "Sultan", a ruler from the Arab world. This reflects the use of imagery of the *Arabian Nights* elsewhere in Maud, and also shows how the narrator and Maud have established a series of private jokes. They mean that he is pompous, autocratic, and used to getting his own way. The very pronounced use of the internal feminine rhyme of "vext her and perplext her" emphasizes how Maud has been upset by her brother's criticism, as well as showing that this is a satirical piece of writing.

Her brother has mainly criticized Maud for avoiding her "little lazy lover", the new-made lord. The "l" sounds and the dismissive word "little" emphasize the narrator's contempt for the lord. Maud has also not shown enough affection towards the lord; the "coldness of her manners" and the "plainness of her dresses" have shown her lack of interest. The narrator admits that he has only ever seen Maud in two outfits, a "habit, hat and feathers" and a "frock and gipsy bonnet". The narrator does not care about luxurious dress. The breathless cluster of internal rhymes that finish the stanza seems to mock the brother's interest in what Maud wears. The narrator doesn't know which of her two normal outfits is "neater and completer", because "nothing can be sweeter / Than maiden Maud in either". This shows that the narrator feels he and Maud are above frivolous things such as clothes and luxuries.

The second stanza opens with an odd phrase: "But tomorrow, if we live". This is ominous. In the midst of a seemingly satirical section about the brother and the new-made lord, we see a sense of death intruding again into the poem. This is typical of the very sharp changes of tone in Maud. We learn that the following day the "ponderous squire" – or Maud's fat brother – will give a "grand political dinner" to the local gentry. The narrator calls them "squirelings". To add the suffix "ling" to a noun in old English was known as a "diminutive" ending; this means therefore "little squires". It is a very dismissive way of talking about them. Imagining the dinner causes the narrator to become increasingly emotional: he starts three lines with "And", breathlessly describing what will happen when Maud appears, when she will "wear her jewels".

The narrator uses animal metaphors to describe the brother and the new-made lord. He calls the brother "the bird of prey". This means, like an eagle or a hawk, he will circle around. It also is a sinister image, because a bird of prey is hunting. Here, he is hunting the new-made lord, to catch him and his money by marrying off Maud to him. The new-made lord is described as the prey of such a bird. He is a "titmouse" or very small rodent. This implies he is very small and weak-willed and in danger from Maud's brother. The narrator laughs at the new-made lord's attempts to win Maud, carrying on with the animal metaphor. He imagines that "the titmouse [will] hope to win her / With his chirrup at her ear". The word "chirrup" is onomatopoeic, representing the squeak of a mouse. This metaphor makes the new-made lord seem unmanly, and carries on the satirical tone of the section.

### 3

A grand political dinner
To the men of many acres,
A gathering of the Tory,
A dinner and then a dance                    *820*
For the maids and marriage-makers,
And every eye but mine will glance
At Maud in all her glory.

### 4

For I am not invited,
But, with the Sultan's pardon,                *825*
I am all as well delighted,
For I know her own rose-garden,
And mean to linger in it
Till the dancing will be over;
And then, oh then, come out to me             *830*
For a minute, but for a minute,
Come out to your own true lover,
That your true lover may see
Your glory also, and render
All homage to his own darling,                *835*
Queen Maud in all her splendour.

Synopsis

The narrator is not invited to the political dinner, but he is planning to hide in the rose-garden at Maud's house, and then invite her to sneak out to meet him after the dancing is over. .

Stanzas 3-4

Stanza three opens with a repetition from stanza two to set the scene: "A grand political dinner". The stanza then continues to discuss who is attending this event. There will be "the men of many acres / A gathering of the Tory". This means that people who are owners of large amounts of land will be there, an acre being a measure of land (equivalent to 0.4 hectares). The word "Tory" is used in the modern day in the United Kingdom to mean supporters of the Conservative Party, which is a modern right-wing political party, with a core belief in low taxation, free markets, and preservation of tradition. The predecessors of the Conservatives were the Tory party, who were the party of large landowners, who sought to protect their rights. Here, the narrator implies they are rich and powerful by using this word, in contrast to his humble, poverty-stricken state.

The dinner will be followed by a dance; at the dance, another form of deal might be struck, because there will be "maids and marriage-makers there". The word "marriage-maker" is another way of saying "matchmaker", who are people in the 19th century who would arrange marriages between important families. The implication is that there will be an attempt to arrange Maud's marriage to the new-made lord. The narrator is not invited to either the dinner or the dance. He imagines wistfully that "every eye but mine / Will glance at Maud in all her glory".

The final stanza of this section, stanza four, reveals the narrator's plan for the evening. He cannot resist a final jibe at Maud's brother, calling him once more the Sultan. The narrator explains how he means to hoodwink Maud's brother: "I know her own rose-garden, / And mean to linger in it". His plan is to wait until after the dance, and then invite Maud out to meet him secretly. The narrator uses repetition very powerfully in the following lines: "And then, oh then, come out to me / For a minute, but for a minute / Come out to your own true lover, / That your true lover may see / Your glory also". This repetition is very musical, and could be seen to represent dance music playing, as well as showing the strength of the narrator's emotion.

The stanza ends with an image of Maud as Queen: she is "Queen Maud in all her splendour". This shows that the narrator worships here, paying homage as a subject would to their monarch.

The symbolic use of the rose in the rose-garden, with its poetic meanings of desire and death throughout the poem *Maud*, will be taken up and developed in the short section twenty-one which follows these stanzas.

## XXI

RIVULET crossing my ground,
And bringing me down from the Hall
This garden-rose that I found,
Forgetful of Maud and me,                    *840*
And lost in trouble and moving round
Here at the head of a tinkling fall,
And trying to pass to the sea;
O Rivulet, born at the Hall,
My Maud has sent it by thee                   *845*
(If I read her sweet will right)
On a blushing mission to me,
Saying in odour and colour, "Ah, be
Among the roses to-night."

Synopsis

The narrator is back at his house, waiting before he ventures to the Hall to wait in Maud's rose-garden. He notices that the small stream that flows from Maud's house through to his property has carried a rose along with it. He imagines that Maud has sent it to him as a secret message, in order to remind him to come and meet her after the dance.

Verse Form

The feminine rhymes from the satirical section twenty have been abandoned in favour of more conventional single-syllable rhymes, more suited to a very lyrical and emotionally charged section. The stanza is composed of thirteen syllables; a traditionally unlucky number; this odd-numbered length might symbolize and foreshadow dark events in the rest of the poem. The lines remain short, with three stressed syllables, and an unobtrusive but subtle and effective rhyme-scheme, with no rhyming couplets.

Stanza 1

The poem is addressed to the "rivulet", a small stream which flows from Maud's house through the narrator's property, down to the sea. The rivulet has carried with it a "garden-rose" from Maud's house. It is important that the word "garden-rose" is used rather than wild rose, as this makes it plain that the rose has not simply come from elsewhere on its journey, but is a cultivated variety. What is happening to the rose is symbolic. It is "lost in trouble and moving round / Here at the head of a tinkling fall, / And trying to pass to the sea". This means it is caught, and being buffeted at a small waterfall. The phrase "lost in trouble" is very ominous, and is symbolic of the obstacles that have been placed between Maud and the narrator, and it foreshadows the tragic events of the rest of the poem. A rose in trouble could be seen to be an omen of a troubled love to come.

(The word "tinkling" in the description of the small waterfall above is a use of onomatopoeia, in that it cleverly mimics the sound of the stream).

The stanza continues, after this bad omen of the rose battered by the current, with another direct address to the stream. Now, the narrator imagines that the rose did not arrived by accident, but was sent by Maud as a message to him, "on a blushing mission" to tell him to come to the Hall. The way this is expressed emphasizes the eroticism of the rose symbol. The phrase "blushing mission" hints at Maud's sexual arousal. The rose's sensual impact is stressed, as it seems to speak to the narrator "in odour and colour". The stanza ends with what the rose seems to be saying, "Ah, be / Among the roses tonight." The enjambment between these two lines gives a further vivid emphasis.

On one level, this means simply come to the rose-garden. However, the use of "rosy" as an adjective for Maud's lips, and section seventeen's linkage of Maud's mouth with a rose, means that to be among the roses sounds like a euphemism for kissing Maud, or, even more sexually, implies that the narrator is imagining having sex with Maud, as the focus on the rose-red colour of Maud's lips and mouth is a veiled way of talking about her vagina.

1

COME into the garden, Maud,
  For the black bat, night, has flown,
Come into the garden, Maud,
  I am here at the gate alone;
And the woodbine spices are wafted abroad,
  And the musk of the roses blown. *855*

2

For a breeze of morning moves,
  And the planet of Love is on high,
Beginning to faint in the light that she loves
  On a bed of daffodil sky,
To faint in the light of the sun she loves, *860*
  To faint in his light, and to die.

3

All night have the roses heard
  The flute, violin, bassoon;
All night has the casement jessamine stirr'd
  To the dancers dancing in tune; *865*
Till a silence fell with the waking bird,
  And a hush with the setting moon.

4

I said to the lily, "There is but one
  With whom she has heart to be gay.
When will the dancers leave her alone? *870*
  She is weary of dance and play."
Now half to the setting moon are gone,
  And half to the rising day;
Low on the sand and loud on the stone
  The last wheel echoes away. *875*

5

I said to the rose, "The brief night goes
  In babble and revel and wine.
O young lord-lover, what sighs are those,
  For one that will never be thine?
But mine, but mine," so I sware to the rose, *880*
  "For ever and ever, mine."

Synopsis

At dawn, after waiting in the rose garden all night during the dinner at Maud's house, the narrator calls to Maud to come and see him. The narrator imagines speaking to the lily and the rose in this garden.

Verse Form

This section of *Maud* is the most famous, as it was adapted into a hugely popular song during Tennyson's lifetime. It could be turned into a song easily, as it is very lyrical. It is composed of fairly regular stanzas – between six and eight lines – and the line lengths remain equal (four stress per line) with a regular rhyme scheme, ABABAB(AB). The easy, flowing verse form stresses the narrator's happiness and anticipation at seeing his beloved.

Stanza 1-5

The first stanza repeats its first and third lines: "Come into the garden, Maud", to show the narrator's persistence in wishing Maud were there. The narrator uses the metaphor of a "black bat" to discuss the night, which has "flown" to be replaced by morning. The sinister bat – the harsh "b" alliteration emphasizing its ominous nature – has been replaced by the light of morning, which symbolizes how Maud has transformed the narrator's life. The narrator then concentrates on the smells of the night, and their sensual nature. The gentle "w" sounds in the "woodbine spices are wafted abroad" mimic the soft breeze. The first use of rose imagery comes here, with the "musk of the roses blown". The word "musk" here introduces a first sexual note; a musky smell is a strong scent, often used in perfumes; it is a type of powerful, dark smell used by plants or animals to attract a mate.

Stanza two continues with this erotic undertone in the description of the dawn. The "planet of love" or Venus, the morning star, is fading in the growing sunlight. Venus is the goddess of love from classical mythology. This image shows how the narrator sees everything, even the night sky, in terms of his love for Maud. The whole stanza continues with erotic imagery. The narrator watches the planet Venus grow dimmer in the sunlight: "faint in the light that she loves / On a bed of daffodil sky". The word "bed" carries a sexual meaning, and the word "faint" is repeated three times, imagining Venus overpowered by the sun's rays. The phrase "the light that she loves" is also repeated, again stressing overwhelming love. The final lines "To faint in his light, and to die" imagine Venus dying for love in the sun's rising. Orgasm used to be described as a "little death", and there is an echo of this in the description of Venus and the sun. It also shows, as throughout Maud, the themes of love and death and entwined.

Stanza three imagines the roses hearing the sound of the music, and jessamine (jasmine) stirred by the dancers inside. Then "a silence fell with the waking bird, / And a hush with the setting moon". This stanza serves mainly to establish how long the narrator has kept his vigil, as it repeats "All night" at the start of lines one and three. Quietness (in the words "hush" and "silence") is contrasted with the sound of the "flute, violin, bassoon" – the instruments of the band.

Stanzas four and five introduce the two key flowers used as symbols throughout Maud: the lily, and the rose; the narrator addresses both in turn, confiding his fears and hopes to then.

In Stanza four, the narrator complains to the lily that Maud is "weary of dance and play", and wishes to be left alone, as she only loves the narrator: "There is but one / With whom she has heart to be gay". This stanza is longer than the first four, at eight lines, the extra length symbolizing the boredom of the narrator waiting, and Maud weary with the dance going on too long. The last four lines concentrate on the guests leaving, building up the suspense of the narrator: half the guests leaving at night, the other half leaving at "the rising day". Finally all of them are gone: "Low on the sand and loud on the stone / The last wheel echoes away", leaving the narrator waiting alone for Maud.

As the lily represents virginity and purity in *Maud*, the rose symbolizes sexual love, violent emotion, and sometimes death; in the fifth stanza, addressed to the rose, the narrator's emotions therefore run much higher than in the lily verse before it. The narrator focuses here on the "babble and revel and wine" of the dance, with the word "babble" using onomatopoeia to depict the party's hubbub. The narrator, jealously, imagines the "young lord-lover", his rival, sighing for "one that will never be thine" – namely Maud. The narrator's jealousy and possessiveness come out in the repetitive and emphatic final two lines: Maud is "But mine, but mine", the narrator tells the rose, concluding with a statement that Maud will always belong to him: "For ever and ever, mine."

## 6

And the soul of the rose went into my blood,
  As the music clash'd in the hall;
And long by the garden lake I stood,
  For I heard your rivulet fall         *885*
From the lake to the meadow and on to the wood,
  Our wood, that is dearer than all;

## 7

From the meadow your walks have left so sweet
  That whenever a March-wind sighs
He sets the jewel-print of your feet         *890*
  In violets blue as your eyes,
To the woody hollows in which we meet
  And the valleys of Paradise.

## 8

The slender acacia would not shake
  One long milk-bloom on the tree;         *895*
The white lake-blossom fell into the lake,
  As the pimpernel dozed on the lea;
But the rose was awake all night for your sake,
  Knowing your promise to me;
The lilies and roses were all awake,         *900*
  They sigh'd for the dawn and thee.

Synopsis

The narrator continues to wait for Maud in the garden. In his imagination, the narrator recalls his walks with Maud in meadows and woods; as he waits in the garden, he imagines the flowers (in particular lilies and roses) are sharing his vigil.

Stanzas 6 -8

Stanza six continues with the rose image of stanza five. He uses it to describe his increasing emotional excitement: "the soul of the rose went into my blood, / As the music clash'd in the hall". The word "clash'd" is an odd choice of word. It implies a discord, or unpleasant sound; the narrator we recall was not invited, and here he is showing how he is out of step with those inside, celebrating. The image of the rose entering his blood means that he is filled up with the intensity of his love, and could also mean he is sexually aroused. But blood also has a sinister connotation of death in *Maud*. The reader must recall the opening of the whole poem, in which the "blood-red heath" surrounds the hollow where the narrator's father died. Once more, in the midst of descriptions of love and desire, there is an allusion to death.

The stanza then moves to describe the natural world. The narrator is standing by the lake in Maud's garden, listening to the rivulet or stream of section twenty-one, which flows from the Hall through to the narrator's house in the wood, via a meadow. The wood is "dearer than all", made special by Maud's presence. Stanza seven continues to describe this landscape, but in much more fanciful terms, as the narrator as carried away by his love for Maud to use a number of extravagant similes. Maud's walks through the meadow have transformed the landscape, the very footprints where she trod turned into flowers: "whenever a March-wind sighs / He sets the jewel-print of your feet / In violets blue as your eyes". This is a use of personification, making the wind itself into a character who praises Maud and almost magically creates beauty. There is a use of hyperbole, or overstatement, at the end of this stanza. The valleys where the narrator walks with Maud have also been transformed and are now "the valleys of Paradise". This stanza shows how far from reality the narrator is moving, as his longing for Maud grows more intense.

Stanza eight, like stanza four, is longer at eight lines in total. This extra length is taken up with even more use of flower-imagery. We see the blossom of acacia trees, and the pimpernel. The importance of these two flowers lies in their colours: the acacia blossom is a "long-milk bloom", or "white lake-blossom"; the pimpernel has another name, scarlet pimpernel, showing it is bright red. These echo the colours of the main two symbolic flowers, the lily and the rose, but the acacia and pimpernel play a different and less important role, as they merely set the scene. The atmosphere created by the descriptions of the acacia blossom and the pimpernel is drowsy, and very sensual; the "slender acacia" does not want to move, its white blossom dropping lazily into the lake; the pimpernel "dozed on the lea", representing the sleep that the narrator has denied himself.

When the lily and the rose are reintroduced, we see the narrator linking the two together, and they seem to accompany the narrator in his vigil: "But the rose was awake all night for your sake, / Knowing your promise to me". The narrator then says the lily was with him too: "The lilies and roses were all awake / They sigh'd for the dawn and thee". The red and the white flowers represent the narrator balancing two impulses here: between seeing Maud as pure and good and spiritual (the white lily), and seeing Maud as the object of his sexual desire (the red rose) – a desire which might lead to death in its violent passion.

## 9

Queen rose of the rosebud garden of girls,
  Come hither, the dances are done,
In gloss of satin and glimmer of pearls,
  Queen lily and rose in one; 905
Shine out, little head, sunning over with curls,
  To the flowers, and be their sun.

## 10

There has fallen a splendid tear
  From the passion-flower at the gate.
She is coming, my dove, my dear; 910
  She is coming, my life, my fate;
The red rose cries, "She is near, she is near;"
  And the white rose weeps, "She is late;"
The larkspur listens, "I hear, I hear;"
  And the lily whispers, "I wait." 915

## 11

She is coming, my own, my sweet,
  Were it ever so airy a tread,
My heart would hear her and beat,
  Were it earth in an earthy bed;
My dust would hear her and beat, 920
  Had I lain for a century dead;
Would start and tremble under her feet,
  And blossom in purple and red.

Synopsis

The narrator continues to describe Maud according to the symbolic associations of the lily and the rose, uniting their spiritual and emotional meanings in a series of vivid images. The stanza – and part one of the poem – ends with a violent image that imagines the narrator's love surviving death, pointing forwards to the disturbing scenes of madness in section two.

Stanzas 9 – 11

Stanza nine develops the synthesis of lily and rose in the person of Maud, as in stanza eight, as both the spiritual and sexual sides of the narrator's desire are expressed in further hyperbolic images. Maud is now the "Queen of the rosebud garden of girls". She is in "gloss of satin and glimmer of pearls, / Queen lily and rose in one". Again, she unites white and red images, in the red rosebud, and the white satin and pearls. The narrator then compares her to the sun itself: "Shine out, little head, sunning over with curls, / To the flowers, and be their sun." It could be argued that the narrator is losing a grip on the reality of Maud, and is over-idealizing her; there is no sense here of Maud's own feelings, as she becomes a focus for the narrator's incredibly poetic language.

A number of additional flowers are introduced as symbols in stanza ten. We see the return of the passion-flower from section fourteen, with its associations of the suffering of Christ and echoes of death. Here a "splendid tear" falls, which is an odd adjective, as we do not usually associate tears with being splendid, rather they are usually sad. This alerts us to take what the narrator says with some skepticism. A further religious image comes when Maud is described as a "dove", a bird with symbolic associations of peace, but also representing the Holy Spirit in the Christian Trinity. Maud is therefore seen as extremely spiritual, and the narrator further idealizes her. She is in the narrator's words "my life, my fate". The red rose is then introduced, crying "She is near, she is near", which is balanced by a white rose, who "weeps" and cries "She is late". This is the first negative image – she might not actually be coming. The next flower – the larkspur – listens and calls "I hear, I hear". The larkspur is a native English flower, and was seen to denote fickleness, again introducing a note of doubt. The narrator, though, concludes the stanza with the steadfast, pure lily, which whispers "I wait".

These flower symbols have therefore created a very emotionally charged atmosphere in the poem, in which the conflict between purity and desire are expressed in the different flowers, with their different symbolic meanings. The final stanza, stanza ten, abandons flower imagery, for something more powerful and disturbing. The stanza opens with a sense of hope: "She is coming, my own, my sweet". Even if she had "so airy a tread", the narrator would still hear her. But the stanza then takes a much more sinister turn. The narrator would hear her come and his heart would beat "Were it earth in an earthy bed". This means even if the narrator were dead. The narrator's heart, even if long-since buried and turned to dust, would beat as if he had "laid for a century dead". The final image picks up the red colour, used throughout the section in relation to the rose, and makes it horrifying: the narrator's buried heart "Would start and tremble under her feet, / And blossom in purple and red." There is a grim pun in "blossom" here, which means open like a flower, but here means the buried heart bleeding out into the ground. After this section's lengthy series of highly stylized flower images, the narrator has returned to the imagery of gothic horror which opened *Maud* itself. (The famous song version "Come into the garden, Maud" omits from its final verse the "century dead" and "blossom in purple and red" lines, as these move the poem into the unpleasant and upsetting themes that will dominate part two).

Part one of *Maud* therefore both starts and ends with an image of blood; the opening of section one imagined the place where the narrator's father died, "dabbled with blood-red heath", dripping "with a silent horror of blood". Now, the narrator's love for Maud is so all-engrossing, the image he choose to express this love imagines his long-buried dead heart would "blossom in purple and red". As throughout *Maud* love and death and two sides of the same desire.

This is a clever way for Tennyson to bring this section to an end, and points towards the developments of part two, in which we learn the tragic consequences of what happened to the narrator in the garden; these final lines foreshadow the narrator's fate, and are an ironic foreshadowing of the madness which will befall him.

"THE FAULT was mine, the fault was mine"—
Why am I sitting here so stunn'd and still,
Plucking the harmless wild-flower on the hill?—
It is this guilty hand!—
And there rises ever a passionate cry                    *5*
From underneath in the darkening land—
What is it, that has been done?
O dawn of Eden bright over earth and sky,
The fires of Hell brake out of thy rising sun,
The fires of Hell and of Hate;                           *10*
For she, sweet soul, had hardly spoken a word,
When her brother ran in his rage to the gate;
He came with the babe-faced lord;
Heap'd on her terms of disgrace,
And while she wept, and I strove to be cool,             *15*
He fiercely gave me the lie,
Till I with as fierce an anger spoke,
And he struck me, madman, over the face,
Struck me before the languid fool,
Who was gaping and grinning by:                          *20*
Struck for himself an evil stroke;
Wrought for his house an irredeemable woe
For front to front in an hour we stood,
And a million horrible bellowing echoes broke
From the red-ribb'd hollow behind the wood,             *25*
And thunder'd up into Heaven the Christless code,
That must have life for a blow.
Ever and ever afresh they seem'd to grow.
Was it he lay there with a fading eye?
"The fault was mine," he whisper'd, "fly!"              *30*
Then glided out of the joyous wood
The ghastly Wraith of one that I know;
And there rang on a sudden a passionate cry,
A cry for a brother's blood:
It will ring in my heart and my ears, till I die, till I die.   *35*

Synopsis

Part two opens with the narrator sitting alone on a hillside, guilty for what he has done. He remembers the night he waited in the garden. Maud came to see the narrator, but her brother and the new-made lord surprised the couple. Maud's brother spoke to her harshly, and struck the narrator. The narrator and Maud's brother have a duel in the wood, and the narrator kills Maud's brother. The dying brother forgives the narrator and urges him to flee; Maud arrives, sees her dead brother, and screams, a sound that the narrator will never forget.

Verse Form

This section is compose of two stanzas – the first at thirty-five lines, the longest yet in the poem. The verse is very irregular, reflecting the chaotic state of mind of the narrator. Line lengths vary between six and fifteen syllables, expanding as the narrator recalls the horror of that night, and leaving pauses or ellipses to intrigue the reader.

Stanza 1

The poem opens with a quotation, but as yet we do not know who was speaking. This creates an air of mystery; we do not know yet either when this section immediately follows on: "The fault was mine, the fault was mine" implies a terrible event. The reader is kept further in suspense, as the narrator seems baffled by where is: "Why am I sitting here so stunn'd and still, / Plucking this harmless wild-flower on the hill?" The wanton destruction of a "harmless wild-flower" is followed by an emphatic: "It is this guilty hand", and the line ends suddenly. This gap is called an ellipsis – and the reader is encouraged here to imagine what awful event has happened.

The narrator does not yet mention what his guilty of, but uses a number of striking images to show how he is horrified by his own actions. He imagines a "passionate cry / From underneath in the darkening land"; a mysterious voice seems to cry to the narrator "What is it, that has been done?" This is perhaps the voice of the narrator's own conscience, which in his imagination he gives to nature itself, as what he has done is so unnatural it causes nature to reject him. As the voice seemed to come from "underneath", the narrator perhaps imagines it is Hell itself which is calling. He contrasts this to the "dawn of Eden" which is the sun rising, but he is obsessed by Hell, as his crime is so great: "The fires of Hell brake out of thy rising sun, / The fires of Hell and of Hate". By withholding narrative details, and using powerful biblical imagery, Tennyson causes suspense and dread in the reader.

The rest of stanza one returns us to the events at the end of part one, section twenty-two, when the narrator was waiting for Maud. Lines eleven to twenty-two are mainly narrative, with sparing use of poetic techniques. Maud, however, is described as a "sweet soul", the sibilance of these words stressing her kindness, and spiritual qualities, when confronted with the violence that is unfolding. Maud's brother and the new-made lord surprise them, and Maud's brother abuses her verbally, then physically assaults the narrator by striking him in the face. The word "struck" is repeated three times: this creates an effect of onomatopoeia, the harsh "st" and "k" of the monosyllabic word sounding like a slap. Other clever uses of sound heighten the dramatic scene, like the picture of the "languid fool", or new-made lord, "gaping and grinning", where the alliteration and half-rhyme have a grimly comic effect. There is a pun as well in the line "Struck for himself an evil stroke", where the word stroke means both the blow landed by Maud's brother, but also recalls the phrase a "stroke of luck". As we learn, it is bad luck for the brother.

A duel takes place an hour later. The narrator here returns to the very start of the poem; in a very gothic image, the hollow where the narrator's father died seems to call out to the narrator for revenge: "a million horrible bellowing echoes broke / From the red-ribb'd hollow behind the wood". The repeated "l" sounds in the first line reinforce the sense of echoing sound, and the word "red-ribb'd" implies there will be blood spilt. Instead of the Christian message of turning the other cheek, the narrator is possessed by the "Christless code, / That must have life for a blow". Then the narrator seems to lose control of himself, and there is a mysterious gap in the narrative, as if the narrator had succumbed to rage and madness: suddenly the brother is seemingly dying in front of him, which surprises the narrator: "Was it he lay there with a fading eye?" The opening lines of the stanza become clear: "The fault was mine" are not the narrator's, but are the brother's dying words. Then Maud appears, described in terms of a ghost: out of the "joyous wood", she comes, "The ghastly Wraith of one that I know". This seems to imply that Maud is already doomed – as she is already a ghost. Maud lets out "A cry for a brother's blood", and the narrator know he will be haunted by this sound: "It will ring in my heart and ears, till I die, till I die". The repetition of this final phrase – like a bell sounding – cleverly shows how this will stay with the narrator forever.

Is it gone? my pulses beat—
What was it? a lying trick of the brain?
Yet I thought I saw her stand,
A shadow there at my feet,
High over the shadowy land.     *40*
It is gone; and the heavens fall in a gentle rain,
When they should burst and drown with deluging storms
The feeble vassals of wine and anger and lust,
The little hearts that know not how to forgive:
Arise, my God, and strike, for we hold Thee just,     *45*
Strike dead the whole weak race of venomous worms,
That sting each other here in the dust;
We are not worthy to live.

Synopsis

The narrator has just seen a ghost. He debates whether he really saw it, or whether it was just an illusion created by his own mind. The narrator then wishes God would strike him down, alongside other weak humans who give in to anger and their worst emotions.

Stanza 2

In a much shorter second stanza in this section, Tennyson continues to mix shorter lines with longer lines, especially to show the narrator rising to a peak of emotion. He uses another key feature of the first stanza – questions – in order to show the narrator's confusion. The first two lines contain three questions in rapid succession: "Is it gone? My pulses beat – / What was it? A lying trick of the brain?" The first question also implies a narrative gap between stanzas: we have to work out that the narrator has seen a ghost, whom we later learn is a "she". (We have not been made aware of Maud's fate yet, though it would be a reasonable assumption to assume it is her.) All of these questions make us as readers uncertain as well as to what has happened, both to Maud and the narrator; the phrase "trick of the brain" also calls into question both the sanity, and the reliability, of the narrator here. The long dash after "My pulses beat" is a clever use of punctuation to show the narrator's nervous and questioning state of mind, as he pauses as if frightened by what he sees and cannot understand.

The word "beat" echoes its use in section twenty-two, in which it stood for the narrator's heart beating eternally, even beyond death, for the love of Maud. Here instead it shows the physical fear that the narrator feels, when he sees the mysterious figure: "I thought I saw her stand, / A shadow there at my feet, / High over the shadowy land". We can interpret this figure as a ghost, because the word shadow, and its related term shade, is often synonymous with the word ghost. (We should also recall here that the last time the narrator has described Maud, as she found her brother dead, she was already seen as a "ghastly Wraith", which are other words which mean ghost.) It is not yet clear whether the narrator knows if Maud is alive or dead, and in section two of this part, he imagines her alive.

Once more the narrator tries to find an echo of his feelings in the natural world. Throughout part one, Tennyson used the pathetic fallacy, where a writer describes nature in terms that mirror a character's feelings. Here, though, nature appears calm, not tormented like the narrator. The ghost is gone, and it starts raining, but the pleasant rain does not express the violence of the narrator's emotions: "the heavens fall in a gentle rain / When they should burst and drown with deluging storms / The feeble vassals of wine and anger and lust". A vassal means a servant or slave; here it means the narrator himself, who has been carried away by anger to kill Maud's brother, losing control of himself in his rage. He becomes a slave to his own anger. The narrator goes on to criticize humanity further, describing himself as one of the "little hearts that know not how to forgive". This means he recognizes that he should not have fought the duel, in which he killed Maud's brother to avenge an insult.

This violent social criticism echoes the opening stanzas of part one, especially the extensive list of human frailties laid out in section four of part one. In section four, the narrator, before finding a certain happiness in his love for Maud, described human beings as "a little breed". He used an unpleasant image taken from nature to describe the dark thoughts that lurk in people: "each man walks with his head in a cloud of poisonous flies". Now, the narrator uses a similarly disturbing animal metaphor. He asks that God to "Strike dead the whole weak race of venomous worms / That sting each other here in the dust". This metaphor means that the narrator considers all humans to be no better than low, poisonous creatures, and that society is simply a brutal battle for survivors amongst predators. After this extravagant, frightening image, the narrator suddenly introduces a simple, short and terrifying sentence: "We are not worthy to live". This also implies that the narrator is suicidal.

By returning to the same types of image found part one, section four, Tennyson has cleverly shown the narrator trapped again within his own obsessive, self-destructive thoughts. The hope that the narrator had found, in his idealized love for Maud, has proven deceptive, and he is again prey to depression, madness, and delusions.

## II

### 1

SEE what a lovely shell,
Small and pure as a pearl,                       *50*
Lying close to my foot,
Frail, but a work divine,
Made so fairily well
With delicate spire and whorl,
How exquisitely minute,                          *55*
A miracle of design!

### 2

What is it? a learned man
Could give it a clumsy name.
Let him name it who can,
The beauty would be the same.                    *60*

### 3

The tiny cell is forlorn,
Void of the little living will
That made it stir on the shore.
Did he stand at the diamond door
Of his house in a rainbow frill?                 *65*
Did he push, when he was uncurl'd,
A golden foot or a fairy horn
Thro' his dim water-world?

### 4

Slight, to be crush'd with a tap
Of my finger-nail on the sand,                   *70*
Small, but a work divine,
Frail, but of force to withstand,
Year upon year, the shock
Of cataract seas that snap
The three-decker's oaken spine                   *75*
Athwart the ledges of rock,
Here on the Breton strand!

Synopsis

The narrator is now on a beach in Brittany, northern France. He looks at a tiny, but beautifully formed shell; he imagines the creature that once inhabited the shell, but now is dead. However frail the shell seems, it has withstood years of storms.

Verse Form

Section two is mainly composed of lines of three firm stresses, with a variable number of unstressed syllables. This makes the verse form fluid, but with a strong sense of underlying structure, at least at the start of the section; this echoes the meaning, which talks about the fragile but strong and symmetrical sea-shell. As the section develops, both stanza length and line length increase, as often in *Maud*, to show growing emotion on the narrator's part.

Stanzas 1-4

Stanza one opens with an imperative form of the verb, commanding the reader: "See what a lovely shell, / Small and pure as a pearl". This simile compares the shell to a precious pearl, describing its beauty and whiteness, even though it cost nothing. It is "Frail, but a work divine", meaning that its beauty comes from God. It is made "fairily well", which means as if crafted by fairies, or magical creatures. The narrator continues to focus on it, especially its "delicate spire and whorl". This means it is twisted, and thin like the spire of a church. It is "exquisitely minute, / A miracle of design!" This focus upon a beautiful example of nature seems to distract the narrator from his gloom of the previous section. The rhyme scheme in this small stanza mirrors the beautiful design of the shell. The rhyme "shell" and "well" are similar to the half-rhyme "pearl" and "whorl", which are further echoed in the "l" sounds that run through this stanza: "small", "lovely", "frail", "fairily", etc. This regularity and careful sound patterning accentuate the sense of symmetry and beauty in the description of the shell.

Stanza two reflects upon the limits of knowledge and science. The narrator does not know its real name, but is certain a "learned man could give it a clumsy name", presumably a lengthy Latin name. The short second stanza ends with a statement: "Let him name it who can, / The beauty would be the same". This is an allusion to a similar statement in Shakespeare's *Romeo and* Juliet, in which Juliet dismisses the fact Romeo is a Montague, not a Capulet, by saying that his name is meaningless: "A rose by any other name would smell as sweet" (Act II, Scene II). This allusion – to a play in which lovers are tragically thwarted by families in conflict – is a clever way that Tennyson shows how the narrator is always thinking of Maud and his own family tragedy.

Indeed, stanza three shifts to one of the narrator's key obsessions: death. The shell is no longer inhabited: "The tiny cell is forlorn, / Void of the little living will / That made it stir on the shore". The word "cell" introduces a sinister note of being locked up. The narrator continues to imagine the world of the creature, and uses a number of very extravagant metaphors to describe the creature who used to live in the shell: the unknown creature opens his "diamond door" wearing a "rainbow frill", and when uncurled he imagines the creature pushing a "golden foot" or a "fairy horn" through the water. These images show that narrator nostalgically imagining a lost world of splendour; again, this could be read as a metaphor for his own lost world, destroyed by his anger and the duel after the dance.

Stanza four returns to the theme of resilience. The shell might be "Slight, to be crush'd with a tap / Of my finger-nail on the sand", but it remains "a work divine". It has therefore an unexpected strength to withstand the force of nature. The narrator uses an image that compares its strength to that of ships which are wrecked by the waves on the shores of Brittany. He uses enjambment to mimic the effects of the waves. The shell has the "force to withstand, / Year upon year, the shock / Of cataract seas that snap / The three-decker's oaken spine / Athwart the ledges of rock, / Here on the Breton strand". A cataract means a waterfall – here, the sea is so strong and waves so high they seem to fall vertically. The ship (a "three-decker") is made of wood, and personified as having an "oaken spine", which is snapped by the sea. This is a violent and effective set of images, made more vivid by the "s" sounds, whose sibilance echoes the sounds of sea, in "shock", snap", "seas", "spine" and "strand". We could interpret this theme – that the seeming frail can be very strong – as hopeful, in that the damaged and depressed narrator could be talking about himself, and his ability to survive the terrible events of his life.

## 5

Breton, not Briton; here
Like a shipwreck'd man on a coast
Of ancient fable and fear—                     *80*
Plagued with a flitting to and fro,
A disease, a hard mechanic ghost
That never came from on high
Nor ever arose from below,
But only moves with the moving eye,            *85*
Flying along the land and the main—
Why should it look like Maud?
Am I to be overawed
By what I cannot but know
Is a juggle born of the brain?                 *90*

## 6

Back from the Breton coast,
Sick of a nameless fear,
Back to the dark sea-line
Looking, thinking of all I have lost;
An old song vexes my ear;                      *95*
But that of Lamech is mine.

## 7

For years, a measureless ill,
For years, for ever, to part—
But she, she would love me still;
And as long, O God, as she                     *100*
Have a grain of love for me,
So long, no doubt, no doubt,
Shall I nurse in my dark heart,
However weary, a spark of will
Not to be trampled out.                        *105*

Synopsis

The narrator bemoans the fact he is exiled in France. He sees a ghostly figure resembling Maud, but reasons it is only an illusion, not a genuine ghost from either heaven or hell. The narrator believes that Maud is still alive, and because of this he keeps some sense of hope alive that she still loves him.

Stanzas 5 – 7

The narrator makes it clear he is in Brittany in France, not Britain. He then likens himself to someone shipwrecked, very much like the title character in Defoe's famous novel *Robinson Crusoe* (1719). He is "Like a shipwreck'd man on a coast / Of ancient fable and fear". The terror, though, arises not from his isolation, but from the strange apparition he sees. He discusses this vision using metaphors of disease, as he reasons the ghost arises from mental illness. He is "plagued", for example, with this "disease", which is a "juggle born of the brain", meaning it is literally a delusion of the mind. The word "juggle" is unexpected, and usually used in throwing and catching, but here vividly illustrates how thrown out of kilter the narrator feels.

The other types of metaphor used are very physical, rather than spiritual. It is a "hard mechanic ghost", which means it seems to move mechanically, following the narrator's own line of vision: it "only moves with the moving eye / Flying along the land and the main", meaning it moves along the horizon as the narrator scans it. The ghost, or whatever it is, is not in the narrator's view of supernatural origin: it "never came from on high / Nor ever arose from below". The narrator is keen to assign it an earthly origin, but this could be because he is in denial that Maud is dead: "Why should it look like Maud?" he asks himself, but there is only one reason why a ghost should look like Maud: and that is Maud is no longer alive. The narrator finishes this stanza with a display of bravery, asking why he should be "overawed" by a mere illusion.

Stanza six picks up the use of illness imagery from stanza five. The narrator is "Sick of a nameless fear". We do not know what this fear is, but it is likely it is the fear he has permanently lost Maud. He carries on to say he is "Looking, thinking of all I have lost", the use of the present participles here showing he is trapped in a state which does not end. There is a use of the pathetic fallacy in the fact the sea mirrors his dark mood, in the "dark sea-line" of the horizon.

*Maud* has often used Biblical allusions to show the narrator's feelings. Here, there is another reference to the Bible, the Old Testament book of Genesis. The narrator fixates on an old song which annoys him, but he then says that "that of Lamech is mine". In the Bible, Lamech was a descendant of Cain, son of Adam. Cain was cursed for killing his brother in a fit of jealousy. Lamech also killed a man, and felt himself even more cursed than his poor ancestor. In Genesis 4.22, Lamech says "If Cain shall be avenged sevenfold, truly Lamech seventy and sevenfold". This means that Lamech's punishments shall be many times worse that Cain's: and Cain's punishment was to be exiled. This reference to Lamech's curse shows how guilty the narrator feels about the possible murder of Maud's brother, and how he regards his current exile in France as part of his punishment for this rash act, and that he knows he is embarking on a long period of suffering.

Stanza seven opens therefore with a sense of the endless nature of the narrator's future torment. He repeats the phrase "For years" in lines one and two, realizing he will suffer a "measureless ill", or endless pain, in being kept apart from Maud forever. The narrator though does not give up hope. He focuses on the possibility Maud might still have "a grain of love for me". The use of the word "grain" here means something very small, like a grain of rice; if there is still something there, the narrator will "nurse" the tiny hope in his "dark heart". He then uses a metaphor taken from kindling fire; he will keep in his heart "However weary, a spark of will / Not to be trampled out". This means he will protect the flame of his hope, believing there is a small chance of reconciliation with Maud.

## 8

Strange, that the mind, when fraught
With a passion so intense
One would think that it well
Might drown all life in the eye,—
That it should, by being so over-wrought,                     *110*
Suddenly strike on a sharper sense
For a shell, or a flower, little things
Which else would have been past by!
And now I remember, I,
When he lay dying there,                                       *115*
I noticed one of his many rings
(For he had many, poor worm) and thought
It is his mother's hair.

## 9

Who knows if he be dead?
Whether I need have fled?                                      *120*
Am I guilty of blood?
However this may be,
Comfort her, comfort her, all things good,
While I am over the sea!
Let me and my passionate love go by,                          *125*
But speak to her all things holy and high,
Whatever happens to me!
Me and my harmful love go by;
But come to her waking, find her asleep,
Powers of the height, Powers of the deep,                     *130*
And comfort her tho' I die.

Synopsis

The narrator is surprised that he is able to focus on little things, such as a shell or a flower, in the face of such intense passion. He remembers that Maud's brother was wearing a ring of his mother's hair as he lay dying. However, the final stanza of the section shows the narrator changing his mind, and saying he is no longer sure the brother did die. He ends the stanza with a plea to the heavens to look Maud, away over the sea.

Stanzas 8 – 9

The narrator opens stanza nine with an observation. The opening word "Strange" sets up a tone of bemusement. He cannot believe that he is able to notice little objects when in the grip of violent emotion, when he is "fraught / With a passion so intense / One would think that it well / Might drown all life in the eye". The image that passion might "drown" all other images is a violent one, and shows that the narrator is always thinking of death. However, the opposite is true, it seems to sharpen the senses. The narrator uses sibilance here to express his surprise at this: using the repeated "s" sound to accentuate his message, that the eye might "Suddenly strike on a sharper sense / For a shell, or a flower". The "s" sounds also picks up the opening "s" of "Strange".

The narrator is drawn back into the violent events of the duel. He remembers when Maud's brother "lay dying there" that the brother was wearing a ring made of his and Maud's mother's hair. Rings made of human hair were very popular in the Victorian period, and were worn by people who were mourning the death of loved ones. This detail humanizes Maud's brother, who had only been seen in very negative terms by the narrator. He, like Maud and the narrator, had lost a mother. The narrator now calls him "poor worm", which is a strange image to use; here it means a lowly creature, but also it emphasizes how close to death was the brother, soon to be buried, his body given over to the earth and to decay. Again, it shows the obsession with death that has overtaken the narrator, as well as showing his sympathy and pity for the brother.

A feature of the second part of *Maud* is the speed at which the narrator changes his mind. After talking sympathetically about Maud's dying brother, the narrator suddenly questions whether the brother died at all. The narrator uses a rapid series of questions, showing his fickle and unfocussed mind: "Who knows if he be dead / Whether I need have fled? / Am I guilty of blood?"

The narrator then returns, equally rapidly and abruptly, to thoughts of Maud. He addresses himself to "all things holy and high" to protect Maud while he is away. The short, three-stress lines are replaced with longer, more emotional outbursts, with more used of repetition, as in: "Comfort, her, comfort her, all things good / While I am over the sea!" He realizes that he must stay away from Maud. He initially expresses this as "Let me and passionate love go by", but this changes a few lines later to a sober realization he is the cause of all the trouble: "Me and my harmful love go by".

The stanza ends with three lines which are almost like a lullaby in their soothing, balanced rhythm: "But come to her waking, and find her asleep, / Powers of the height, Powers of the deep, / And comfort her tho' I die". The word "die" ends this stanza on a sombre note; and, as we recall, sleep can be equated with death in *Maud*, as sleep was called in part one, section eighteen a "false death". This gentle but ominous ending to part two, section two prepares us for the shocking revelations of section three, in which the narrator reveals the truth about Maud's fate.

# III

COURAGE, poor heart of stone!
I will not ask thee why
Thou canst not understand
That thou art left for ever alone: *135*
Courage, poor stupid heart of stone.—
Or if I ask thee why,
Care not thou to reply:
She is but dead, and the time is at hand
When thou shalt more than die. *140*

Synopsis

The narrator realizes he has been deluding himself that Maud is still alive; he finally admits that she is dead. The knowledge she is dead will have a devastating effect on the narrator.

Verse Form

The verse is similar to the preceding section; most lines have three stresses, with an additional stress included in a longer line, when the narrator's emotions are heightened. Two rhymes are repeated: "stone" and "why". This repetition of the same word shows the narrator is trapped in his grief.

Stanza 1

The whole stanza takes the form of an address to the narrator's own heart. This shows a battle between his reason (which knows that Maud is dead) and his emotions (which are denying this fact, to protect him). The narrator's reason shows pity for his own predicament: "Courage, poor heart of stone!" We would expect a "heart of stone" to be a metaphor showing someone has no emotions, but here the implication is that the narrator's heart is not stony or cold, but simply unable to comprehend the enormity of loss.

Tennyson is cleverly re-using a metaphor to give it further depth. The central metaphor of a "heart of stone" was used in part one, section six, in which the narrator talked about his sad life before Maud. The death of his father and his poverty led to a childhood marked by a "morbid hate and horror" of the world, which had given him a "heart half-turn'd to stone". This led to the narrator choosing to be alone, and to reject love. Maud's reappearance gave him new life: "O heart of stone, are you flesh, and caught / By that which you swore to withstand?" The "heart of stone", or rejection of emotion, was a means of protecting the young narrator, but Maud had got through his defences. Here, though, the narrator's rational side realizes this protection will be inadequate, now that Maud is gone.

The narrator continues to take pity on himself: "I will not ask thee why / Thou canst not understand / That thou are for ever alone". Dividing himself into his rational and his emotional side shows the narrator remains aware of the difference between truth and delusion, but this sense of division hints at the potential for the narrator to lose control of his sanity and his grasp on reality. He repeats his plea to his own heart to be brave: "Courage, poor stupid heart of stone." (The introduction of the word "stupid" shows the narrator knows that the denial of the truth cannot continue.)

The narrator knows that it is perhaps better that his heart does not reply to his rational mind's questions, because the truth is so terrible: "if I ask thee why, / Care not thou to reply". The final lines, increasing in length and stress to show the weight of emotion, finally admit Maud's fate: "She is but dead, and the time is at hand / When thou shalt more than die". This is a terrible prediction for the narrator to give on himself. What does it mean to "more than die"? This points forward to a period of awful suffering for the narrator, which resembles the old cliché of "a fate worse than death".

The division between the narrator's rational mind, and his emotional heart, is key to this stanza and its role in the development of the plot in *Maud*. The narrator risks losing his mind completely and descending into madness due to the intensity of his grief and guilt. The calm shown here is a brief respite before the "grief and pain" of the next few sections.

## IV

### 1

O THAT 'twere possible
After long grief and pain
To find the arms of my true love
Round me once again!

### 2

When I was wont to meet her
In the silent woody places
By the home that gave me birth,
We stood tranced in long embraces
Mixt with kisses sweeter sweeter
Than anything on earth.

### 3

A shadow flits before me,
Not thou, but like to thee;
Ah Christ, that it were possible
For one short hour to see
The souls we loved, that they might tell us
What and where they be.

### 4

It leads me forth at evening,
It lightly winds and steals
In a cold white robe before me,
When all my spirit reels
At the shouts, the leagues of lights,
And the roaring of the wheels.

### 5

Half the night I waste in sighs,
Half in dreams I sorrow after
The delight of early skies;
In a wakeful doze I sorrow
For the hand, the lips, the eyes,
For the meeting of the morrow
The delight of happy laughter,
The delight of low replies.

Synopsis

The narrator wishes he could feel Maud's arms around him once more, and recalls their embraces in the woods. He sees Maud's ghost regularly, leading him through the unnamed and terrifying city in which he is now living, while he spends the rest of his time pining for what he has lost, and day-dreaming about Maud.

Verse Form

This section contains much of the most poignant verse in Maud. It is composed of short, lyrical lines of three stresses, most falling into loose iambic hexameters. Rhyme is unobtrusive but fairly regular and stanza lengths vary from four to eight lines (usually six). Only occasional long lines trouble a fairly unified mood of deep sadness.

Stanza 1 -5

The first stanza was written many years before the publication of *Maud*. It was first composed in 1833-34, just after the death of Tennyson's beloved friend Arthur Hallam, and re-used in 1837 in a very early version of this part of *Maud*. The poetic techniques are simple, with only the heartfelt "O" and the exclamation mark at the end of the stanza standing out. The narrator wishes he could find the arms of his "true love" around him again. The genuine grief of Tennyson on Hallam's death lends the whole of this section tremendous power.

The next stanza returns to the memories of Maud, and the landscape round the Hall. He remembers that he used to meet her in "the silent woody places" nearby. The narrator uses a metaphor taken from hypnotism, to describe how he they "stood tranced in long embraces". This means they forgot about everything while they kissed. The feminine rhyme of "places" and "embraces" shows the strength of emotion this memory awakens. The embraces were "Mixt with kisses sweeter sweeter / Than anything on earth". The word "sweeter", repeated and emphasized by its witty feminine rhyme with "meet her", introduce a note of lightness and joy; we recall that "sweet" and "sweeter" are adjectives always associated with Maud, in the more innocent and playful sections of part one of the poem.

More typical of part two's darker tone is an abrupt change of town in stanza three, with the reappearance of the ghost: "A shadow flits before me, / Not thou, but like to thee". The narrator knows it is not Maud in reality, just a "shadow", which brings him no comfort in the vision. He calls out to Jesus for help; he wishes that he had knowledge to know what happens to loved ones after their death. This shows he has no faith in Maud going to heaven, rather he does not want to know what will happen. Tennyson's typical technique of the odd, startling long line to show emotion is used, in his wish "to see / The souls we loved, that they might tell us / What and where they be."

In the next stanza, we are back in terrible city, after the sweet memories of the wood. The ghost draws the narrator out into the crowds at evening. It "lightly winds and steals / In a cold white robe" in front of the narrator. A white robe here means a winding-sheet, which is a cloth in which the dead are buried. The use of "winds" is a grim pun on this. The narrator is buffeted by the sounds of the city. His spirit "reels / At the shouts, the leagues of lights, / And the roaring of the wheels". The "r" sounds in "reels" and "roaring" mimic the hubbub of the street scene, and the "leagues of lights" illustrate the vastness and confusion of the modern city. The word "roaring" is a word usually taken from nature, to describe the sound of the lion, or of the wind; here it shows the terror of the seemingly normal traffic to the disturbed, haunted narrator.

The narrator's life in the city is caught between sleeping and waking, between the comforting memories of the past, and the awful present. This conflict is cleverly expressed in the repetition of "Half" at the start of lines one and two of stanza five: "Half the night I waste in sighs, / Half in dreams I sorrow after / The delight of early skies". He therefore spends his team wishing he were back with Maud. He is in a "wakeful doze". There is a powerful use of the word "sorrow" here as a verb, which is not usual in modern English. The stanza ends with a list of all he has lost with the death of Maud; her "hand, the lips, the eyes", the promise of meeting her, and in the poignant last lines he recalls that he lost her voice: "The delight of happy laughter, / The delight of low replies". Repetition here of the word "delight" shows the strength of passion that the narrator has, which will in the next stanza lead him to relive the final moments of the "meeting of the morrow" that lead to her brother's death and the narrator's exile.

6

'Tis a morning pure and sweet
And a dewy splendour falls
On the little flower that clings
To the turrets and the walls;
'Tis a morning pure and sweet,                    *175*
And the light and shadow fleet;
She is walking in the meadow,
And the woodland echo rings;
In a moment we shall meet;
She is singing in the meadow,                      *180*
And the rivulet at her feet
Ripples on in light and shadow
To the ballad that she sings.

7

Do I hear her sing as of old,
My bird with the shining head,                     *185*
My own dove with the tender eye?
But there rings on a sudden a passionate cry,
There is some one dying or dead,
And a sullen thunder is roll'd;
For a tumult shakes the city,                      *190*
And I wake, my dream is fled;
In the shuddering dawn, behold,
Without knowledge, without pity,
By the curtains of my bed
That abiding phantom cold.                         *195*

Synopsis

In a dream, the narrator relives the morning he waited for Maud to meet him after the dance. This happy memory is shattered by the narrator recalling Maud's terrible cry at discovering her brother dying, and the narrator awakens to see Maud's ghost standing by his bed.

Stanzas 6 – 7

The narrator suddenly shifts into the present tense. We are in the midst of a dream in which he is reliving the final morning he spent with Maud. Stanza six is wholly positive in tone. It is a lost idyll or paradise. The first line, "'Tis a morning pure and sweet" is repeated in line five, emphasizing the purity and wholeness of this vision. We return to the flower imagery of the end of part one: "a dewy splendour falls / On the little flower that clings / To the turrets and the walls". Here, the word shadow is not a sinister synonym for ghost, but merely a normal part of the natural world, part of the morning: "'Tis a morning pure and sweet / And the light and shadow fleet". The word "fleet" means fast moving, meaning the sun is coming up quickly.

Maud appears in the narrator's dream, again in the present tense: "She is walking in the meadow, / And the woodland echo rings". The narrator mixes together here many of the key descriptions or incidents of part two, creating a composite image of Maud at her most beautiful. She is "singing in the meadow" which recalls the time he watched her singing a "passionate ballad" in part one, section five. There is a "rivulet at her feet", like the stream which runs from the Hall to the narrator's house, carrying the rose she sends as a message, in part one, section twenty-one. The echo of the "r" sounds between "rivulet" and "Ripples" echoes the sounds of the water, adding to the sense that this is a scene of great calm and beauty.

Stanza seven starts very much like the previous stanza, with a memory of Maud's singing. The narrator describes her as a bird, a "dove", which is a symbol of peace and happiness: "Do I hear her sing as of old, / My bird with the shining head, / My own dove with the tender eye?" This peace is shattered, though, by the narrator remembering the terrible outcome of his duel with Maud's brother, and his death at the narrator's hands.

For the second time in this section, a much longer line expresses a sudden emotional outburst, as the narrator awakens from his dream: "But there rings on a sudden a passionate cry, / There is someone dying or dead". The sounds here are those of the present day, of the terrible city in which the narrator now lives: "And a sullen thunder is roll'd; / For a tumult shakes the city, / And I wake, my dream is fled".

The narrator is in his bed in the present day. He wakes alone in the "shuddering dawn". The word "shuddering" means to tremble uncontrollably; here it shows that the narrator has awoken terrified. The unpleasant alliteration on the "d" sounds accentuates the horror the narrator feels at what he sees – and his sadness at waking from the dream, which had been so comforting and pleasant until the "passionate cry" rang out.

The narrator has been sleeping in a four-poster bed, which would have curtains drawn around it. The narrator, through these curtains, sees an awful sight, the ghost of Maud. This ghost is "Without knowledge, without pity", which means it seems to have no consciousness or desire to communicate with the narrator. It is a "phantom cold", simply following him. The narrator, before and after this, seems to realize that the apparition is not real, simply a manifestation of his state of guilt and mental illness.

## 8

Get thee hence, nor come again,
Mix not memory with doubt,
Pass, thou deathlike type of pain,
Pass and cease to move about,
'Tis the blot upon the brain          *200*
That *will* show itself without.

## 9

Then I rise, the eavedrops fall,
And the yellow vapours choke
The great city sounding wide;
The day comes, a dull red ball          *205*
Wrapt in drifts of lurid smoke
On the misty river-tide.

## 10

Thro' the hubbub of the market
I steal, a wasted frame,
It crosses here, it crosses there,          *210*
Thro' all that crowd confused and loud
The shadow still the same;
And on my heavy eyelids
My anguish hangs like shame.

Synopsis

The narrator tells the ghost to leave him alone. He seems to know that it is simply a figment of his imagination. The narrator gets up and wanders through the city, and the ghost follows him.

Stanzas 8 – 9

Stanza eight opens with the narrator addressing the ghost directly. He uses six verbs in the imperative form, which is used to give orders: "Get thee hence", "nor come", "Mix not", "Pass" (repeated), and "cease". This shows him trying to re-establish rational control over his emotions. He tells the ghost to go and leave him permanently. The apparition causes him pain by mixing "memory with doubt". This means causing him to remember the terrible events at the Hall, and to doubt that Maud is dead, which leads him to get false hope. He realizes that the ghost is not real. It is only a "deathlike type of pain", arising from inside his body. The narrator reiterates this by describing it as a "blot upon the brain / That will show itself without". Again, this means he know it is only an external symbol of his internal struggle, and a delusion. The word "blot" usually means an ink stain; here the metaphor means that the narrator's mind has been darkened and coloured indelibly by Maud's death.

The narrator, in stanzas nine and ten, tells of his typical, monotonous days in the city. The city is described in very different terms form the countryside of part one. He rises from his bed when water is dripping from the gutters, when "the eavesdrops fall, / And the yellow vapours choke / The great city sounding wide". In the 19th century, great cities such as London were affected badly by smog, a mixture of smoke and fog, which caused many deaths and respiratory diseases. The fog was often described as yellow, as it contained many particles form the many coal fires that burnt through the city. Clean air legislation in the mid 20th century finally stopped smog in the United Kingdom.

The rest of stanza eight continues to describe the city in vivid, and unreal terms. The sun is a "dull red ball / Wrapt in drifts of lurid smoke / On the mist river-tide". Though we are never told if the city is London, this description resembles many representations of the great city in art and literature in the 19th century, in which fog accentuates the dirtiness and decay. Charles Dickens, in his great novel *Bleak House* (1853), describes it thus: "Fog everywhere. Fog up the river, where it flows among green aits and meadows; fog down the river, where it rolls defiled among the tiers of shipping and the waterside pollutions of a great (and dirty) city."

The choking vapours and lurid smoke are also an example of the pathetic fallacy; the narrator's mental confusion is expressed in the unpleasant descriptions of nature.

In stanza ten, we move into the life of the city, into its markets: "Thro' the hubbub of the market / I steal, a wasted frame". The word "hubbub" is an example of onomatopoeia, mimicking the sounds of the crowds. The narrator is a "wasted frame", made thin and unhealthy by guilt and lack of sleep, but also "wasted" in the sense that he has wasted his life and his love. The ghost still follows him through the masses of people, an internal rhyme of "crowd" and "loud" drawing attention to the narrator's distress: "It crosses here, it crosses there, / Through all that crowd confused and loud / The shadow still the same".

The stanza ends with the narrator guilty and upset by what he has done. This is expressed by the use of a metaphor of anguish weighing on the narrator's "heavy eyelids [...] like shame". This also expresses the narrator's lack of sleep, due to his disturbed dreams.

### 11

Alas for her that met me,
That heard me softly call,
Came glimmering through the laurels
At the quiet evenfall,
In the garden by the turrets
Of the old manorial hall.

### 12

Would the happy spirit descend,
From the realms of light and song,
In the chamber or the street,
As she looks among the blest,
Should I fear to greet my friend
Or to say "Forgive the wrong,"
Or to ask her, "Take me, sweet,
To the regions of thy rest"?

### 13

But the broad light glares and beats,
And the shadow flits and fleets
And will not let me be;
And I loathe the squares and streets,
And the faces that one meets,
Hearts with no love for me:
Always I long to creep
Into some still cavern deep,
There to weep, and weep, and weep
My whole soul out to thee.

Synopsis

The narrator feels sorry that Maud ever came to see the narrator on the fateful evening at the Hall, which started the whole tragic chain of events that led to her brother's death and to her death. The narrator wishes that the genuine spirit of Maud would descend from heaven, looking beautiful like other inhabitants of paradise, and then he would ask for her forgiveness. However, the shadow that does accompany him, as a delusion from his own brain, allows him no such comfort. The section ends with the narrator wishing he could hide away from the unfriendly, hostile city and cry out to Maud for forgiveness.

Stanzas 11 – 13

Stanzas eleven and twelve move from the grim present to a more comforting world for the narrator. In stanza eleven, the narrator expresses regret that Maud ever met him on the final night at the Hall Garden. The language reflects the beauty of the countryside, in stark contrast to the ugly town. The narrator remembers Maud who "Came glimmering through the laurels / At the quiet evenfall / In the garden by the turrets / Of the old manorial hall." This "quiet" of the evening is another strong contrast to the "hubbub of the market" in the previous stanza, which so torments the narrator, and the word "glimmering" stresses Maud's beauty and lightness, as opposed to the city's dark, foggy melancholy.

The narrator, in stanza twelves, wishes that he could really meet the spirit of Maud rather than the delusion caused by his madness. She would be a "happy spirit", coming "From the realms of light and song". Again, there is a contrast between the harmony and light of heaven, and the noise and murk of the city. The narrator would like to see Maud as she is "among the blest", namely as would appear as in heaven. He would then be able to address her directly without fear, and ask for forgiveness. He would also be able to ask her to take him to heaven with her: "Take me, sweet, / To the regions of thy rest". This means he would ask to die; it is an example of the narrator showing his desire to commit suicide.

The final stanza abruptly snaps the narrator out of this comforting daydream. It opens with the conjunction "But", sharply bringing us back to reality, and the true nature of the ghost that haunts the narrator. Stanza thirteen's rhyme scheme is also very clever, and uses the same vowel sound – a long "e" – in every single rhyme of the ten lines. There are also many repetitions and slight variations of the rhyme words. This creates a sense that the verse is not moving forward or changing, and the narrator is trapped in a vicious circle, haunted by his guilt.

The stanza opens with the word "beats", picking up a use of this word in the section which described the narrator's terrified heartbeat when seeing the ghost. The next section will develop this word and theme further. Here, the ghost will not let the narrator rest, under the city's streetlamps: "But the broad light glare and beats / And the shadow flits and fleets / And will not let me be". The alliteration of "flits and fleets" accentuates the narrator's nervous exhaustion. More sentences begin with "And", showing the narrator's agitation as the terror his life increases, and the lines tumble out of him: "And I loathe the squares and streets, / And the faces that one meets, / Hearts with no love for me". As noted, the rhymes and assonances "beats", "fleets", "me be", "streets", "meets" and "me" allow no variety, and also mimic the narrator's own terrified heartbeat.

The final four lines take the repletion of the long "e" sound further, in describing the narrator's desire to escape from the city, to find a silent place to mourn Maud: "Always I long to creep / Into some still cavern deep, / There to weep, and weep, and weep / My whole soul out to thee". The repetition of "weep" shows the narrator's depth of pain, but the cleverest use of sound here is the three repeated "o" sounds in the final line, in "whole soul out". This sounds like someone howling in pain. The image of a "cavern deep" points forward to the next section, in which the narrator imagines himself dead and speaking from beyond the grave.

V

1

DEAD, long dead,
Long dead!                                                              *240*
And my heart is a handful of dust,
And the wheels go over my head,
And my bones are shaken with pain,
For into a shallow grave they are thrust,
Only a yard beneath the street,                                         *245*
And the hoofs of the horses beat, beat,
The hoofs of the horses beat,
Beat into my scalp and my brain,
With never an end to the stream of passing feet,
Driving, hurrying, marrying, burying,                                   *250*
Clamour and rumble, and ringing and clatter,
And here beneath it is all as bad
For I thought the dead had peace, but it is not so;
To have no peace in the grave, is that not sad?
But up and down and to and fro,                                         *255*
Ever about me the dead men go;
And then to hear a dead man chatter
Is enough to drive one mad.

2

Wretchedest age, since Time began,
They cannot even bury a man;                                            *260*
And tho' we paid our tithes in the days that are gone,
Not a bell was rung, not a prayer was read;
It is that which makes us loud in the world of the dead;
There is none that does his work, not one;
A touch of their office might have sufficed,                            *265*
But the churchmen fain would kill their church,
As the churches have kill'd their Christ.

Synopsis

The narrator has gone mad, and is locked in a lunatic asylum. He believes he is already dead and buried below the ground, though he can hear everything in the outside world. He believes his fellow patients are also the living dead.

Verse Form

Section five of part two is the most irregular of all the poem, reflecting the narrator's madness: lines range from two syllables up to fourteen syllables, and stanzas from four to twenty lines.

Stanzas 1-2

Stanza one opens with two very short lines: "Dead, long dead, / Long dead!" This could refer to Maud or Maud's brother, but we are shocked to discover it is in fact the narrator himself. He imagines himself already turned to dust, in a shallow grave under the road: "And my heart is a handful of dust, / And the wheels go over my head, / And my bones are shaken with pain". This alludes back to the end of part one, at the height of the narrator's intense passion for Maud, when he swears he would love Maud forever. The narrator had said "My heart would hear her and beat, / Were it earth in an earthy bed; / My dust would hear her and beat, / Had I lain for a century dead". What was simply an extravagant image of devotion has become the narrator's delusion, which is a grim irony.

The reuse of the word "beats" from part one becomes the dominant metaphor here: the sound of the passing world is like a terrible heartbeat to the troubled narrator, showing how everything simply adds to his pain: "The hoofs of the horses beat, beat, / The hoofs of the horses beat, / Beat into my scalp and my brain". Tennyson cleverly uses repetition of these words and rhymes to show the narrator's endless torment. He follows his with a very clever use of present participles, showing the activity of the world, which passes the narrator by: "never an end to the stream of passing feet, / Driving, hurrying, marrying, burying". The metaphor streams likens passers-by to a river, which emphasizes their endless flow. The coupling of "marrying, burying" is terrible irony; the narrator wanted to marry Maud, but instead she is now dead. Love and death and also here coupled together, as earlier in the poem.

The next line emphasizes the sounds the narrator hears: "Clamour and rumble, and ringing and clatter". These words are mainly onomatopoeic, or mimic genuine noises. The rest of this stanza describes where the narrator is; in an asylum, surrounded by fellow sufferers from mental illness. The narrator calls his fellow patients as the dead as well. He says it is "sad" that even the dead "have no peace in the grave", but wander around. The final four lines end with a grim irony as well: "up and down and to and fro, / Ever about me the dead men go; / And then to hear a dead man chatter / Is enough to drive one mad". But the narrator is already mad, and locked away from the world, imagining he is already dead. The word "chatter" is another effective use of onomatopoeia; we can imagine the way that the narrator cannot stand the voices of his fellow patients.

In the mid-19th century, conditions in mental hospitals were improving from a low point in the 18th century, when people would pay to look at inmates as entertainment. However they were still large, impersonal places, more concerned with restraint than treatment. The word "bedlam", which means chaos or disorder, comes from the name of Bethlem Royal Hospital in London, and shows how these asylums were objects of fear and popular fascination.

Stanza two is a criticism of contemporary religion. The narrator, in his madness, says it is the church's fault he is trapped with the living dead. Particularly in Roman Catholic countries, religious services are held to pray for the souls of the dead, that they will go to heaven. The narrator says that this doesn't work because modern English churches and priests no longer really believe in God: "the churchmen fain would kill their church / As the churches have kill'd their Christ". The narrator's delusion is that the dead souls trapped in the asylum would have been released to go to heaven if the correct ceremonies has been performed – and which had been paid for in "tithes" or taxes to the church: "And tho' we paid our tithes in the days that are gone, / Not a bell was rung, not a prayer was read; / It is that which makes us loud in the world of the dead". Of course, this is not true; the inmates are all actually alive, but this passage allows Tennyson to criticize the lack of faith in God in the Victorian era, This was also a concern of other writers, such as fellow poet Matthew Arnold, who wrote in *Dover Beach* (1851, published 1867), that the "Sea of Faith" or religious belief, had disappeared, leaving people in state of confusion and distress, with "neither joy, nor love, nor light, / Nor certitude, nor peace, nor help for pain".

## 3

See, there is one of us sobbing,
No limit to his distress;
And another, a lord of all things, praying                    *270*
To his own great self, as I guess;
And another, a statesman there, betraying
His party-secret, fool, to the press;
And yonder a vile physician, blabbing
The case of his patient—all for what?                         *275*
To tickle the maggot born in an empty head,
And wheedle a world that loves him not,
For it is but a world of the dead.

## 4

Nothing but idiot gabble!
For the prophecy given of old                                  *280*
And then not understood,
Has come to pass as foretold;
Not let any man think for the public good,
But babble, merely for babble.
For I never whisper'd a private affair                         *285*
Within the hearing of cat or mouse,
No, not to myself in the closet alone,
But I heard it shouted at once from the top of the house;
Everything came to be known:
Who told *him* we were there?                                  *290*

## 5

Not that gray old wolf, for he came not back
From the wilderness, full of wolves, where he used to lie;
He has gather'd the bones for his o'ergrown whelp to crack;
Crack them now for yourself, and howl, and die.

Synopsis

The narrator describes some of his fellow inmates in the asylum, and the delusions from which they are suffering. The narrator then wonders how Maud's brother came to hear that Maud was meeting the narrator on the fatal evening at the Hall. He reasons it could not be Maud's father, who did not return from abroad.

Stanzas 3 – 5

Stanza three describes fellow patients in the asylum who are suffering from delusions. The opening word, an imperative verb, "See", introduces a series of vivid descriptions. All of the patients are described with a present participle, all forming rhymes or half-rhymes, emphasizing their repetitive, disordered symptoms, and the similarity of their delusions. The first is inconsolable in grief, perhaps even the narrator himself, "sobbing, / No limit to his distress". The second believes himself to be a god, "a lord of all things, praying / To his own great self". The third believes himself to be a corrupt politician talking to the press, "betraying / His party-secret".

The narrator introduces a fourth figure: "a vile physician, blabbing / The case of his patient". The last description is interesting; we are not sure whether the narrator is talking about an inmate who thinks he is a doctor, or is simply describing a doctor treating the patients with a lack of care. This cleverly blurs the distinction between the sane and the insane, and the reader cannot take anything for granted – we do not know who is inmate, and who is doctor.

The futility of trying to understand the delusions of the insane is described by the narrator in a horrible image. What the inmates say is meaningless, and to question them is "to tickle the maggot born in an empty head". Maggots are the larvae of flies, found on dead bodies; this image means the insane can make no sense at all, no more than an insect can make any sense. The doctor's aims at understanding the patients are pointless, because "it is but the world of the dead".

This idea –that nothing makes sense any more – comes to dominate the next stanza, which opens with the key line: "Nothing but idiot gabble!" Gabble is again onomatopoeic, echoing the nonsensical sounds of the mentally ill here. This echoes the word "blabbing" in stanza three, and later in stanza four the narrator reiterates this, repeating the similar word "babble" twice. The narrator mysteriously mentions that a "prophecy given of old / And then not understood / Has come to pass as foretold", but we are given no hint as to what this prophecy is at all. Is it that the narrator is doomed to become insane? The reader is left confused, as the narrator is confused. The confusion continues as the narrator speculates how Maud's brother knew he was waiting for Maud in the Hall Garden, given that he never told "cat or mouse". The stanza finishes with the lines: "Everything came to be known: / Who told *him* we were there?" The narrator does not allow for a simple explanation, that Maud was observed leaving the house, and a suspicious brother followed her; the narrator is showing his lack of rationality here, looking instead for supernatural reasons.

The narrator will not let go of his obsession with finding out how Maud's brother caught them. He wonders whether it is Maud's father, but dismisses it immediately, as he was out of the country. He uses the same image from part one, describing Maud's father as a wolf, emphasizing his vicious, dangerous qualities: "Not that gray old wolf, for he came not back / From the wilderness, full of wolves, where he used to lie".

At this point, the narrator becomes even more incoherent. He continues the metaphor of the wolf, but the meaning is difficult to establish: "He has gather'd the bones for his o'ergrown whelp to crack; / Crack them now for yourself, and howl, and die". The "o'ergrown whelp" refers to his son, Maud's brother. This metaphor seems to mean that Maud's father assembled wealth for his son by swindling the narrator's father, causing his premature death. However, with the death of Maud and Maud's brother, the old man is left alone to reflect on the consequences of his bloody actions which have resulted in the death of his children: hence the words "Crack them now for yourself". The narrator then curses Maud's father, in "howl, and die". This is a very unpleasant and violent set of images, and demonstrates how dark the narrator's thoughts have become in his madness.

Prophet, curse me the blabbing lip,
And curse me the British vermin, the rat;
I know not whether he came in the Hanover ship,
But I know that he lies and listens mute
In an ancient mansion's crannies and holes:
Arsenic, arsenic, sure, would do it,                            *300*
Except that now we poison our babes, poor souls!
It is all used up for that.

7

Tell him now; she is standing here at my head;
Not beautiful now, not even kind;
He may take her now; for she never speaks her mind,            *305*
But is ever the one thing silent here.
She is not of us, as I divine;
She comes from another stiller world of the dead,
Stiller, not fairer than mine.

8                                        *310*

But I know where a garden grows,
Fairer than aught in the world beside,
All made up of the lily and rose
That blow by night, when the season is good,
To the sound of dancing music and flutes:
It is only flowers, they had no fruits,                        *315*
And I almost fear they are not roses, but blood;
For the keeper was one, so full of pride,
He linkt a dead man there to a spectral bride;
For he, if he had not been a Sultan of brutes,
Would he have had that hole in his side?                       *320*

Synopsis

The narrator is increasingly incoherent in his madness and rage. He blames rats for eavesdropping on him, and giving away his plans to meet Maud. He sees Maud's ghost again and cries out to her father to take the apparition away. The narrator then returns to a vision of the Hall Garden, but the original beauty is replaced by an image of Maud as a "spectral bride" and her brother dead with a deadly wound.

Stanzas 6 – 8

The stanza opens with a repetition of the word "blabbing" from stanza four, as the narrator continues to be fixated upon the question of who told Maud's brother about the secret meeting. The narrator curses the informer, as someone with a "blabbing lip". However, the narrator's madness causes him to see the culprit as "the British vermin, the rat". In modern slang, a "rat" means an informer in criminal slang, but here the narrator seems to believe in a delusion that the actual animal was the tell-tale: "I know that he lies and listens mute / In an ancient mansion's crannies and holes". (The reference to the rat perhaps coming from Hanover in Germany refers to a belief in the 18th century that plague-carrying rats came over from the continent, probably from Norway. As an act of political satire, Jacobite opponents of the new Hanoverian King of England, George I, claimed the rats came over in 1714 with George from Hanover. As Maud's brother has also come from abroad to take his birthright, this allusion may reflect the narrator's hatred of the brother).

The stanza ends with the narrator fixated on poisoning the rat; he cries out "Arsenic, arsenic", which is type of deadly poison. However, the narrator then seems to say that rat poison is being used on babies and is all used up. This illustrates the narrator's delusions, but also refers back to part one, section one, in which the narrator ranted that in modern society pharmacists were poisoning their patients, and shopkeepers put deadly additives in food.

Stanza seven addresses Maud's father, and begs him to take away Maud's ghost. The apparition is once more standing by his bed, but is a terrible sight: "Not beautiful now, not even kind". The ghost remains silent, the only silent thing amongst the noise of the inmates in the asylum: "She comes from another stiller world of the dead, / Stiller, not fairer than mine".

The next stanza opens with five beautiful lines; we are given, as a sharp contrast to all the horror of the asylum, an idyllic memory of the Hall Garden. Opening with the conjunction "But" cleverly sharpens the contrast: "But I know where a garden grows, / Fairer than aught in the world beside". (This is an echo of a very famous passage in Shakespeare's play *A Midsummer Night's Dream*, when Oberon says: "I know a bank where the wild thyme blows, / Where oxlips and the nodding violet grows, / Quite over-canopied with luscious woodbine, / With sweet musk-roses and with eglantine".) This establishes a new mood of beauty and calm, and the allusion to Shakespeare's comedy contrasts with the tragic actions of *Maud*.

The stanza continues with the return of the key symbols of the lily and the rose, expressing the tension between purity and lust, or between death and desire: "All made up of the lily and the rose / That blow by night, when the season is good, / To the sound of dancing music and flutes." But then the idyllic scene is tainted; the garden is ultimately sterile, just as Maud and the narrator's love is cruelly cut short: "It is only flowers, they had no fruits". The narrator then realizes the true meaning of the rose as symbol: "And I almost fear they are not roses, but blood". The rose, representing the triumph of violent desire, will lead to disaster and death.

The final four lines of this stanza replay the tragic events of the last night in the Hall Garden, but in a cryptic form. The "keeper" who is "full of pride" is Maud's brother. By surprising Maud and the narrator, and thwarting their love, he ultimately seals the narrator's and Maud's fate: "He linkt a dead man there to a spectral bride". This means Maud was doomed from the moment the brother arrived. It also ironically echoes the contract between the narrator's father and Maud's father, to marry the pair.

The last two lines try to justify the narrator's killing of Maud's brother: "if he had not been a Sultan of brutes, / Would he have had that hole in his side?" The word "Sultan", an Arabian ruler, was used earlier in the poem to describe the brother, stressing his tyrannical nature. The description of the brother with a "hole in his side" after the fatal duel with the narrator is horrible, and returns us back to the nightmarish world of the asylum, after the very brief pastoral description of the Hall Garden.

## 9

But what will the old man say?
He laid a cruel snare in a pit
To catch a friend of mine one stormy day;
Yet now I could even weep to think of it;
For what will the old man say                                325
When he comes to the second corpse in the pit?

## 10

Friend, to be struck by the public foe,
Then to strike him and lay him low,
That were a public merit, far,
Whatever the Quaker holds, from sin;                         330
But the red life spilt for a private blow—
I swear to you, lawful and lawless war
Are scarcely even akin.

## 11

O me, why have they not buried me deep enough?
Is it kind to have made me a grave so rough,               335
Me, that was never a quiet sleeper?
Maybe still I am but half-dead;
Then I cannot be wholly dumb:
I will cry to the steps above my head,
And somebody, surely, some kind heart will come            340
To bury me, bury me
Deeper, ever so little deeper.

Synopsis

The narrator's troubled and confused mind imagines Maud's father finding a dead body in a pit: it is unclear whether this is his son's corpse in the same pit where the narrator's father was found dead, or both Maud and her brother being dead and in the same grave. The narrator that draws a distinction between killing someone in a lawful war (which is not a sin), or murdering someone in a private feud (which is a sin). Part two ends with the narrator, in his madness, asking to be buried even deeper underground.

Stanzas 9 – 11

The narrator opens by asking a question: what would Maud's father say on finding his son and daughter dead? The image of the "pit", which is in the second and the final line of the stanza, could refer to either the pit in which the narrator's father died, or simply to a grave. It is clear, though, that the narrator believes that Maud's father is ultimately to blame. Like a hunter laying a trap, Maud's father "laid a cruel snare in a pit / To catch a friend of mine one stormy day". This "friend" could be either Maud, or the narrator's father. The narrator then says he "could weep" to think of this death. The stanza ends with another question, emphasizing the narrator's confusion: "what will the old man say / When he comes to the second corpse in the pit?" This is very confusing, as the identity of the two bodies is not made clear; it could be either Maud's brother and Maud, or Maud's brother and the narrator's father. The confusion is due to the narrator's state of mind; it also shows that the narrator hold Maud's father responsible for all of the tragedy, dating back to the decision to swindle the narrator's father and cause his suicide.

The next stanza re-introduces a theme that will be picked up in the *Maud* part three, which follows immediately from this section: this is the theme of the legitimacy of war. The narrator draws a distinction between killing in a war, and murdering a private individual. He is talking here about his killing of Maud's brother. The narrator says that killing "the public foe", or one of Britain's enemies, is a "public merit" or good, which is "far […] from sin". As in part one, when the narrator criticized non-conformist preachers for preaching against war, the narrator is critical of "Whatever the Quaker holds" or believes. Quakers were, and still are, against all war. *Maud* had previously contained many passages in praise of war, and this is no exception. However, killing outside of a legal war is murder. It is "the red life spilt for a private blow". This "lawless war" of private vengeance is what has killed Maud's brother, and damned the narrator. However, the idea of a "lawful" war will ultimately prove the narrator's salvation in part three.

The final stanza of this section, stanza eleven, is filled with pathos. It opens with an exclamation, "O", as the narrator cries out in his misery: "O me, why have they not buried me deep enough? / Is it kind to have made me a grave so rough, / Me that was never a quiet sleeper?" This shows a grim humour; the narrator likens death to sleep, but even in his delusion that he is already dead, he can get no rest. He wonders whether he is not actually dead, but only "half-dead"; if so he will wail and ask to be buried even further underground by some "kind heart". The last two lines include a very strong example of enjambment or a broken line, to show how the narrator's sanity has been broken by tragic events: "surely, some kind heart will come / To bury me, bury me / Deeper, ever so little deeper".

This is the lowest point in the "monodrama" of Maud's narrator; he wishes to be dead, buried away from the world, and free from the apparition of Maud who haunts him and prevents him from resting.

# PART III
## VI
### 1

MY life has crept so long on a broken wing
Thro' cells of madness, haunts of horror and fear,
That I come to be grateful at last for a little thing:  *345*
My mood is changed, for it fell at a time of year
When the face of night is fair on the dewy downs,
And the shining daffodil dies, and the Charioteer
And starry Gemini hang like glorious crowns
Over Orion's grave low down in the west,  *350*
That like a silent lightning under the stars
She seem'd to divide in a dream from a band of the blest,
And spoke of a hope for the world in the coming wars—
"And in that hope, dear soul, let trouble have rest,
Knowing I tarry for thee," and pointed to Mars,  *355*
As he glow'd like a ruddy shield on the Lion's breast.

### 2

And it was but a dream, yet it yielded a dear delight
To have look'd, tho' but in a dream, upon eyes so fair,
That had been in a weary world my one thing bright;
And it was but a dream, yet it lighten'd my despair  *360*
When I thought that a war would arise in defence of the right,
That an iron tyranny now should bend or cease,
The glory of manhood stand on his ancient height,
Nor Britain's one sole God be the millionaire:
No more shall commerce be all in all, and Peace  *365*
Pipe on her pastoral hillock a languid note,
And watch her harvest ripen, her herd increase,
Nor the cannon-bullet rust on a slothful shore,
And the cobweb woven across the cannon's throat
Shall shake its threaded tears in the wind no more.  *370*

Synopsis

Part three opens with the narrator seemingly recovered from his madness. Some time has passed since section two; the narrator has seen Maud in a dream. Maud speaks of coming war, and encourages the narrator to take part, saying she is waiting for him. The narrator's mood has lifted at the thought of a just war against tyranny.

Verse Form

After section two irregular and disturbed verse forms, section three returns to a much more regular form, reflecting the narrator's self-professed recovery from despair. There are five stresses in most lines, but the verse is not a regular iambic pentameter, instead including a variable number of extra unstressed syllables, giving eleven to fifteen syllable lines. This gives the verse a regular pulse, but freedom to respond to the narrator's changing moods. (It is an early example of what the later Victorian poet Gerard Manley Hopkins would term "sprung rhythm".)

Stanzas 1 -2

The narrator opens by using an image from nature for his own illness: his life "crept so long on a broken wing", like an injured bird who cannot fly. He alludes to his incarceration in "cells of madness, haunts of horror and fear". However, we learn that his "mood is changed". We learn that this is because he seen Maud in a dream.

The narrator introduces the dream with a lengthy series of allusions to the time of year. It is clearly early summer, because "the shining daffodil dies", which means spring has ended. The beautiful descriptions of nature from part one have returned, in the delightful image of "the face of night is fair on the dewy downs", which balances the "f" sounds of the first half of the verse, with the "d" alliteration in the second, symbolizing nature in harmony.

References to three constellations then come in; previously the narrator had dismissed stars as meaningless "cold fires", with no deeper meaning. Now they are symbolically important. The charioteer (Auriga), Gemini, and the hunter, Orion are all seen. The stars of Gemini, the twins, are described in very beautiful terms, as "glorious crowns". Even when Orion, low in the sky, is described in his "grave", this is a beautifully poetic and melancholy image, rather than sinister metaphor of being buried. The dream of Maud is then described, picking up imagery of the heavens; her arrival is "like a silent lightning under the stars", and she has come accompanied by fellow inhabitants of heaven: "She seem'd to divide in a dream from a band of the blest".

Maud's message is consistent with part one, in which she was heard singing of the glories of war. She tells the narrator of her "hope for the world in the coming wars", and tells the narrator she is waiting for him. She leaves him with a hint of what she wants him to do. She points to the planet Mars, which is named after the Greek god of war, and the planet "glow'd like a ruddy shield on the Lion's breast". The word "ruddy" means red, like the planet, and the Lion's breast (the constellation Leo) could represent the lion on the coat of arms of the British Monarchy.

There has been much debate as to how we should read the narrator's praise for war here – and whether it truly represents Tennyson's own view of the Crimean War - but stanza two seems to be wholly convinced of the goodness of war. It recycles many of the arguments of the first section of part one. Although it was only a dream, it has galvanized the narrator: "And it was but a dream" is repeated, and the narrator admits the dream "lighten'd my despair / When I thought that a war would arise in defence of the right". The rule of the Russian Tsar is called an "iron tyranny". The repeated "d" sounds in the first half of the stanza provide a strong pulse, like a martial drum.

The second half of the stanza picks up a key theme from part one, that peace had corrupted British society, allowing the desire for profit to run rampant. Money has become all important: a just war would stop "Britain's one sold God be the millionaire". He continues that "No more shall commerce be all in all, and Peace / Pipe on her pastoral hillock a languid note". "Peace" had been personified in part one as a negative influence, and this again shows the narrator returning to his old obsessions. It seems odd to modern readers that the narrator criticizes some of the positive effects of peace, such as watching the "harvest ripen" and the "herd increase"; this has led to critics seeing the narrator's enthusiasm for war as simply another type of madness. The stanza ends with a series of images of weaponry which has lain unused, such as rusty cannon-balls, or a cobweb woven across an unused cannon. He uses personification to talk about the cannon, talking of its throat, or the cobwebs shaking like "threaded tears". In this, he is bizarrely trying to get us to feel sorry for unused weapons, which also might show he is still delusional.

### 3

And as months ran on and rumour of battle grew,
"It is time, it is time, O passionate heart," said I
(For I cleaved to a cause that I felt to be pure and true),
"It is time, O passionate heart and morbid eye,
That old hysterical mock-disease should die."                    *375*
And I stood on a giant deck and mix'd my breath
With a loyal people shouting a battle-cry,
Till I saw the dreary phantom arise and fly
Far into the North, and battle, and seas of death.

### 4                                                           *380*

Let it go or stay, so I wake to the higher aims
Of a land that has lost for a little her lust of gold,
And love of a peace that was full of wrongs and shames,
Horrible, hateful, monstrous, not to be told;
And hail once more to the banner of battle unroll'd!
Tho' many a light shall darken, and many shall weep          *385*
For those that are crush'd in the clash of jarring claims,
Yet God's just wrath shall be wreak'd on a giant liar;
And many a darkness into the light shall leap,
And shine in the sudden making of splendid names,
And noble thought be freer under the sun,                    *390*
And the heart of a people beat with one desire;
For the peace, that I deem'd no peace, is over and done,
And now by the side of the Black and the Baltic deep,
And deathful-grinning mouths of the fortress, flames
The blood-red blossom of war with a heart of fire.          *395*

### 5

Let it flame or fade, and the war roll down like a wind,
We have proved we have hearts in a cause, we are noble still
And myself have awaked, as it seems, to the better mind
It is better to fight for the good, than to rail at the ill;
I have felt with my native land, I am one with my kind,     *400*
I embrace the purpose of God, and the doom assign'd.

Synopsis

Over a period of months, Britain moves closer to war with Russia (the Crimean War, 1853-1856). The narrator believes this to be a just cause, and enlists in the army to travel to the war overseas. He believes the war will transform Britain from a corrupt, money-loving country into a nobler place. The narrator gives his fate over to God.

Stanzas 3 – 4

These sections were written while Britain was preparing for war with Russia, whose territorial aims throughout Europe and Asia threatened British interests. *Maud* was published in 1855, alongside Tennyson's most famous poem about that war, *The Charge of the Light Brigade*, in which both the stupidity and nobility of battle was described; however, in *Maud*, the depiction of war seems wholly positive, though there are hints of another reading.

In stanza three, the months leading up to the war are described. The narrator believes the cause to be "pure and true", and it prompts him to make a decision to choose to leave behind his madness. He uses the device of addressing his own "heart", showing his attempt to master his illness with his reason. He seems to know he has a tendency to melancholy, talking of his "passionate heart and morbid eye". He describes his illness as his "old hysterical mock-disease". The word hysteria was used in the 19th century to describe mental illness in women, which was thought to arise from their wombs; the narrator here is implying his obsession with Maud was unmanly.

However, it could be argued that the narrator is simply replacing one obsession – Maud – with another: war. He is not cured of his disease, it is simply channeled into a fervour for battle. The narrator ends stanza with an image of standing on a ship's "giant deck" with other soldiers, a "loyal people shouting a battle-cry". There is a mysterious image then of watching a "dreary phantom arise and fly / Far into the north, and battle, and seas of death". This could be bidding farewell to Maud's apparition, replaced by a battle against the Russian foe, deep in the frozen north. But he has simply replaced one apparition with another – the illusion of a glorious battle.

Stanza four opens with a dismissive "Let it go or stay", showing how he no longer is scared of Maud's apparition; he has awoken to a new England which has abandoned shameful peace for noble war, for, "the higher aims / Of a land that lost for a little her lust of gold, / And love of a peace that was full of wrongs and shames". A series of negative adjectives show the narrator's contempt for the old Britain: "Horrible, hateful, monstrous". But the narrator is now carried by military glory – much as he was swept up by Maud's martial song. He dismisses the misery that war will cause, because it will replace the Tsar: "many shall weep / For those that are crush'd in the clash of jarring claims, / Yet God's just wrath shall be wreak'd on a giant liar". The hard "c" sounds emphasize the coming violence. Six of the next eight lines open with "And", as the narrator in his excitement lists the benefits of the conflict, with a regular drum-like rhythm. These benefits include people gaining a reputation for bravery ("the sudden making of splendid names"), oppressed people gaining their freedom ("noble thought be freer under the sun"), and the British people becoming more unified ("And the heart of a people beat with one desire").

However, the stanza ends with a series of images that echo uneasily the first part of Maud. In the Black Sea and the Baltic (two sea-coasts of Russia, the first sea holding the Crimean peninsula, the Baltic having Russia's capital St. Petersburg), there will be "deathful-grinning mouths of the fortress", or the mouths of cannon. The mouth image recalls the dreadful pit with its "blood-red" mouth in the opening lines of *Maud*, showing how the narrator is still trapped in his old obsessions of death. From the cannon "flames / The blood-red blossom of war with a heart of fire". These are the cannons being fired; but using "blood-red blossom" returns us to the image of the red rose, which symbolizes desire and death; again, we can see how the narrator's mind still turns to the same images; he may have directed his attention towards patriotism and battle, but the same morbid obsession with death is present.

The final six lines of *Maud* in stanza five ends with a defiant, almost optimistic tone, as the narrator seems to accept his fate is in God's hands. He describes war "like a wind", a simile which implies it will blow away much that is unclean or ignoble. The narrator only momentarily hesitates, when he says, "myself have awaked, as it seems, to the better mind". The words "as it seems", do show a doubt, but are swiftly followed by a seemingly confident final three lines, in which the narrator says he has chosen to live and die in the service of his country: "I have felt with my native land, I am one with my kind, / I embrace the purpose of God, and the doom assign'd." The word "doom" leaves the reader with some uncertainty; has the narrator really changed, or is he still obsessed by death? It is part of the genius of Tennyson that the seemingly certain ending of *Maud* lends itself to many interpretations.

24979854R00070

Printed in Great Britain
by Amazon